someone else's shoes

by Drew

ETT
ENGLISH TOURING THEATRE

Welcome to this performance of Drew Pautz's *Someone Else's Shoes.*

It's a rare experience to read a new play and know within a couple of scenes that it's something that should be staged. That was certainly my experience with Drew Pautz's *Someone Else's Shoes.*

ETT is known above all for its work on the classics. But since 1993 we've premiered six new plays: Jonathan Harvey's *Rupert Street Lonely Hearts Club,* Marty Cruickshank's *A Difficult Age,* Judith Johnson's *Shellfish,* Jonathan Harvey's *Hushabye Mountain,* Peter Gill's *The York Realist,* and, most recently, Richard Bean's *Honeymoon Suite.*

I've always believed that a theatre company benefits from the relationship between the classic and the new, the historic and the contemporary, and I really hope you enjoy our latest encounter with the modern world.

Do visit our new website and add your comments (www.ett.org.uk).

Stephen Unwin
Director

sunwin@ett.org.uk

PRODUCTIONS

2007	*French Without Tears*
2006	*Mother Courage and Her Children*
	The Old Country
2005	*Hamlet*
	Rosencrantz and
	Guildenstern Are Dead
2004	*Twelfth Night*
	Honeymoon Suite
2003	*Romeo and Juliet*
	John Gabriel Borkman
	Anton Chekhov
2002	*The Boy Who Fell into a Book*
	King Lear
	Ghosts
2001	*The York Realist*
	The Caretaker
	Fool For Love
	Love's Labours Lost
2000	*The Cherry Orchard*
1999	*The Master Builder*
	Don Juan
	Hushabye Mountain
1998	*The Taming of the Shrew*
	A Difficult Age
	Shellfish
1997	*Measure for Measure*
	The Seagull
	Design for Living
1996	*Henry IV Parts I & II*
	The School for Scandal
	Hedda Gabler
1995	*Rupert Street Lonely Hearts Club*
	Macbeth
	The Importance of Being Earnest
	The School for Wives
1994	*No Man's Land*
	As You Like It
	The Beaux' Stratagem
	A Doll's House
1993	*A Taste of Honey*
	Hamlet
	Midsummer Night's Dream

AWARDS

SHAKESPEARE'S GLOBE
SAM WANAMAKER AWARD 2003
Stephen Unwin

CRITICS' CIRCLE AWARD
BEST PLAY
Peter Gill *The York Realist*

SUNDAY TIMES
IAN CHARLESON AWARDS
FIRST PRIZE Mark Bazeley
The Seagull
FIRST PRIZE Alexandra Gilbreath
Hedda Gabler
SECOND PRIZE
Daniel Evans *Ghosts*

TMA THEATRE AWARDS
BEST ACTOR
Timothy West *King Lear*
BEST ACTRESS
Diana Quick *Ghosts*
BEST ACTRESS IN A SUPPORTING
ROLE Emma Cunniffe
The Master Builder
BEST TOURING PRODUCTION
Hedda Gabler
BEST ACTRESS
Kelly Hunter *As You Like It*
BEST ACTOR
Alan Cumming *Hamlet*

MANCHESTER EVENING NEWS
AWARDS
BEST ACTOR IN A VISITING
PRODUCTION
Timothy West *King Lear*
BEST ACTRESS IN A VISITING
PRODUCTION
Diana Quick *Ghosts*
BEST ACTOR IN A VISITING
PRODUCTION Timothy West
The Master Builder
BEST NEW PLAY
Rupert Street Lonely Hearts Club
BEST ACTOR
Bette Bourne
The Importance of Being Earnest

WHATSONSTAGE.COM AWARDS
BEST SUPPORTING ACTOR Richard
Coyle *The York Realist*

CITY LIFE AWARD
BEST PLAY
Rupert Street Lonely Hearts Club

CAST
in order of appearance

Adam Amedeo	STEVEN PACEY
Nadine Sanderson	EMILY BRUNI
Richard Amedeo	PATRICK DRURY
Jed Pillar	JONJO O'NEILL
Mary Klemp	DENISE GOUGH

CREATIVE TEAM

DIRECTOR	Stephen Unwin
SET & COSTUME DESIGNER	Anna Fleischle
LIGHTING DESIGNER	Malcolm Rippeth
COMPOSER	Olly Fox
SOUND DESIGNER	Mike Furness
ASSISTANT DIRECTOR	Bethany Ann McDonald
DIALECT COACH	Penny Dyer
CASTING DIRECTOR	Ginny Schiller
PRODUCER	Rachel Tackley

Someone Else's Shoes premiered at Soho Theatre, London, on 8th March 2007

PRODUCTION TEAM

Production Manager	Nick Ferguson/ Matt Noddings
Company Stage Manager	Linsey Hall
Deputy Stage Manager	Jo Keating
Assistant Stage Manager	Emily Oliver
Costume Supervisor	Charlotte Wiseman
Wardrobe Manager	Alex Stewart
Design Assistant	Alice Hoult
Marketing Consultant	Mark Slaughter and Associates
Marketing	Kelly Duffy for Soho Theatre
Press	Nancy Poole for Soho Theatre
Photographer	Stephen Vaughan
Print Design	Jane Harper
Set Built & Painted by	Capital Scenery
Cover Photograph	Manuel Harlan
Logo Design	Ian Fitzsimmons
Work Placement	Reasha Barnes

With thanks to the staff at Soho Theatre,
Gavin and AJ at Café Lazeez, and TEQUILA\ London.

Drew Pautz would like to thank the many who contributed
ideas and support during the writing of this play.
Special thanks to Matthew Dunster, Jennie Darnell,
Joe Phillips and Stephen Unwin for help along the way.

CAST BIOGRAPHIES

EMILY BRUNI
NADINE SANDERSON

Theatre includes: *The Rubenstein Kiss* (Hampstead); *After Mrs Rochester* (Shared Experience); *The Winter's Tale, Camino Real, Much Ado About Nothing* and *The Spanish Tragedy* (RSC).

Television includes: *Catherine the Great, If Africa, Miss Marple – Murder at the Vicarage, Passer-by, Serious and Organised, Believe Nothing, Auf Wiedersehen Pet, Sam's Game, The Scarlet Pimpernel – series 2, Metropolis.*

Film includes: *The Case, Investigating Sex, Being Considered.*

Radio includes: *The French Lieutenant's Woman, The Pallisers, Hecuba, The Woman in White, In the Cage, Learning to Swim, Murder of the Home Front.*

PATRICK DRURY
RICHARD AMEDEO

For ETT: *Mother Courage and Her Children, Hamlet, King Lear, Twelfth Night.*

Theatre: *The Graduate* (national tour); *Dear Daddy* (Ambassadors); *The Memory of Water* (Vaudeville); *Measure for Measure* (Riverside Studios); *The Changeling, The Seagull* and *As You Like It* (Bristol Old Vic); *The Trinidad Sisters* (Donmar); *Flying Blind* and *The Key Tag* (Royal Court); *Prince of Homburg, Don Juan, Danton's Death, Much Ado About Nothing, Torquato Tasso, Fuente Ovejuna, Murderers* (NT); *Coriolanus* (Berkoff); *Afore Night Come* (Young Vic).

Television includes: *Cold Blood,* 3 series of *Father Ted, The Politician's Wife, The Men's Room, Shoot to Kill, Escape Into Thin Air, Inspector Morse, Rumpole, Midsomer Murders.*

Film: *The Awakening, Singleton's Pluck, The Nightingale Saga.*

DENISE GOUGH
MARY KLEMP

Theatre includes: *O go my Man* (Royal Court); *As You Like It* and *The Bog of Cats* (Wyndhams); *The Kindness of Strangers* (Everyman); *Everything is Illuminated* (Hampstead).

Television includes: *Lie With Me, Casualty, The Commander, Inspector Lynley Mysteries.*

CAST BIOGRAPHIES

STEVEN PACEY
ADAM AMEDEO

Theatre includes:
Same Time Next Year
(Sonning); *A
Midsummer Night's
Dream* and *The
Boyfriend* (Regent's
Park); *The Old
Masters* (Comedy);
Democracy (NT); *The
Constant Wife*
(Apollo); *Dolly West's
Kitchen* (Old Vic); *The
Room/Celebration*
(Almeida and New
York); *The Birthday
Party* (Piccadilly);
*Things We Do For
Love* (Gielgud); *By
Jeeves* (Duke of
York's); *Phantom of
the Opera*
(Shaftesbury); *Blithe
Spirit* and *Valentine's
Day* (Chichester);
Exclusive (Strand);
Trelawny of the Wells
(NT); *High Society*
(Victoria Palace);
West Side Story (Her
Majesty's).

Television includes:
*Distant Shores,
Spooks, M.I.T.,
Jeffrey Archer – The
Truth, Murder in
Mind, Nothing but the
Truth, Pipedreams,
Pie in the Sky, Just
William, Lovejoy,
Blake's Seven.*

Film includes: *Return
to House on Haunted
Hill, Conspiracy,
Passover, Aces High,
Julius Caesar.*

JONJO O'NEILL
JED PILLAR

Theatre includes:
Faustus (Hampstead);
*A New Way to Please
You, Believe What
You Will, Sejanus: His
Fall, Speaking Like
Magpies* (RSC);
Head/Case (RSC &
Soho); *Paradise Lost*
(Northampton Theatre
Royal); *A View From
the Bridge* and

Murmuring Judges
(Birmingham Rep);
*Observe the Sons of
Ulster Marching
Towards the Somme*
(The Pleasance); *Dolly
West's Kitchen*
(Leicester Haymarket);
Half a Sixpence (West
Yorkshire Playhouse);
Translations
(Watford); *The Frogs*
(Nottingham
Playhouse).

Television includes:
*The History of Mr
Polly, I Do, The Year
London Blew Up,
I Fought the Law, Bay
College, Murphy's
Law, A Touch of
Frost, Charlie's Angel,
Band of Brothers,
Holby City, Thin Ice,
Extremely Dangerous,
Sunburn.*

Film includes: *Fakers.*

Radio includes:
Whenever and *Poetry
Please.*

CREATIVE TEAM BIOGRAPHIES

STEPHEN UNWIN
DIRECTOR

Founding Director of ETT since 1993.

For ETT: *Mother Courage and her Children, The Old Country* and *Hamlet* (both also in the West End), *Rosencrantz and Guildenstern Are Dead, Twelfth Night, Romeo and Juliet, John Gabriel Borkman, King Lear* (also Old Vic), *Ghosts, Love's Labour's Lost, The Cherry Orchard, The Master Builder, Don Juan, The Taming of the Shrew, A Difficult Age, The Seagull* (also Donmar), *Henry IV Parts I and II* (also Old Vic), *Hedda Gabler* (TMA Best Touring Production, also Donmar), *Macbeth* (also Lyric Hammersmith and Poland), *The School for Wives* (also Riverside Studios), *As You Like It, The Beaux' Stratagem* (also Turkey), *A Doll's House, Hamlet* (also Donmar), *A Midsummer Night's Dream* (also Lilian Baylis).

Theatre: *The Lottery of Love, Torquato Tasso, A Yorkshire Tragedy* (NT Studio as Resident Director); *The Long Way Round* (NT); *The Magic Carpet* (NT Education Department); *Karate Billy Comes Home*; British Premières of *Man to Man* and *The Conquest of the South Pole* (Royal Court); *Elizabeth Gordon Quinn, The Orphans' Comedy, White Rose, Elias Sawney, Abel Barebone* and *Shadowing the Conqueror* (Traverse). London transfers include: *Sandra/Manon* (Donmar); *Kathie and the Hippopotamus* and *White Rose* (Almeida); *Dead Dad Dog* (Royal Court Upstairs). Repertory work includes: *Look Back in Anger* and *Knickers!* (Bristol Old Vic); *Our Country's Good* (Leicester Haymarket); *The Price* (OSC).

Theatre in Europe includes: *Measure for Measure* and *The Comedy of Errors* (Graz); *The Broken Jug* (Antwerp); *Macbeth* (Bochum and Neuss).

Opera: Hans Eisler/Bertolt Brecht's *The Decision* (Almeida Music Festival and Radio Three); *The Marriage of Figaro, Cosi fan Tutte* and *Lucia Di Lammermoor* (Opera 80); *Scipio* (Guildhall School); *Gianni Schicchi* (ENO); *Il Barbiere di Siviglia* (ROH); *Albert Herring, Falstaff, Die Entführung aus dem Serail, Le Nozze di Figaro* and *Don Giovanni* (Garsington Opera).

Writing: *A Pocket Guide to Shakespeare's Plays, A Pocket Guide to Twentieth Century Drama* and *A Pocket Guide to Ibsen, Chekhov and Strindberg* for Faber and Faber, *So You Want to be a Theatre Director?* for Nick Hern Books and *A Guide to the Plays of Bertolt Brecht* for Methuen.

Stephen is Joint Winner of the Shakespeare Globe Sam Wanamaker Award 2003.

CREATIVE TEAM BIOGRAPHIES

DREW PAUTZ
WRITER

Plays for theatre include: *Poor Cousin* (Royal Welsh College of Music and Drama with Hampstead Theatre) and several collaborative writing projects with The Work Theatre Collective, including: *Project E: An Explosion* (also director – BAC) Oxford Samuel Becket Theatre Trust Award; *Project D: I'm Mediocre* (Tristan Bates Theatre); *Project C: On Principle* (TBT/BAC).

Drew has also worked extensively as a lighting designer for both theatre and dance including: *Some Voices* (Young Vic); *Desert* (The Space); *Loser, Night and Day* and *Spike Islands* (Company FZ).

ANNA FLEISCHLE
SET AND COSTUME DESIGNER

Theatre includes: *Love and Money* (Royal Exchange/ Young Vic); *Project B, Project C: 'On Principle'* (BAC), *Project D: 'I'm*

Mediocre' (The Work Theatre Collective); *Dysfunction* (Soho); *Some Voices* (Young Vic); *Attempts On Her Life* (Manchester Metropolitan University); *Prime Location* (Gallowglass Theatre, Ireland); *Jumping On My Shadow* (Theatre Centre); *Macbeth* (Blue Raincoat Theatre, Sligo); *Maria de Buenos Aires* (Vereinigte Buehnen Bozen, Bolzano, Italy); *Unser Dorf Soll Schöner Werden* (West Pfälisches Landes Theater); *The Mousetrap* (Milan); *Celebs* (Old Red Lion); *Weltraum. Faust.Traum* and *The Baa Lambs' Holiday* (Theater K, Aachen); *Cosi, Caberet Verboten, Lovers* and *Into the Darkness Laughing* (New End); *Pains of Youth, Twelfth Night, The Threepenny Opera* and *Allerleiraugh* (Theater Erlangen, Germany).

Dance includes: *Ms Morris* (Intoto Dance Co.); *Trip-Tic* (Mimbre); *Killing Two Birds With One Stone* (film); *Desert* (The Place); *Larynx* (ROH);

Triptych (Sadlers Wells and tour); *See-Saw* (Coventry University and tour); *Porch Time* (ROH Studio and tour); *Babylon, Petrushka, 1052, In Between There Are Doors* and *Querelle de Brest* (Badisches Staatstheater, Karlsruhe, Germany).

Film includes: *Killing Two Birds With One Stone, Fallen Boy/ Dream City.*

Anna trained at Central St Martin's College of Art and Design. She lectures and teaches on all aspects of design in both Germany and the UK and is a founder member of The Work Theatre Collective.

MALCOLM RIPPETH
LIGHTING DESIGNER

For ETT: *Mother Courage, Hamlet* (also West End), *Romeo and Juliet* (also Hong Kong), *John Gabriel Borkman.* As Associate Lighting Designer: *The York Realist* (Strand), *King Lear* (Old Vic).

CREATIVE TEAM BIOGRAPHIES

Theatre includes: *Mrs Warren's Profession* (Edinburgh Lyceum/ Nottingham Playhouse); *Faustus* (Headlong/ Hampstead); *Cymbeline* (Kneehigh Theatre/RSC); *Nights at the Circus* (Kneehigh/Lyric Hammersmith); *The Bacchae, Pandora's Box* (Kneehigh); *Scuffer, The Lion, the Witch and the Wardrobe, Vodou Nation, Homage to Catalonia, Medea* (West Yorkshire Playhouse); *Monkey* (Dundee Rep); *The Little Prince, Great Expectations, Kaput!, The Snow Queen, Noir, Pandora's Box, The Tiger's Bride* (Northern Stage); *Hay Fever, Macbeth* (York Theatre Royal); *A Nightingale Sang in Eldon Square, Our Kind of Fun, Lush Life, Toast, Cooking with Elvis* (Live Theatre); *Coelacanth, Black Cocktail* (Pleasance Edinburgh); *Foyer, The Selfish Giant* (Leicester Haymarket); *Dealer's Choice* (Salisbury Playhouse); *Antigone at Hell's Mouth* (National Youth Theatre) and *Keepers of the Flame* (RSC / Live Theatre). Future projects include *Cyrano de Bergerac* (Bristol Old Vic) and *Tutti Frutti* (National Theatre of Scotland).

Dance includes: *Angelmoth, La Nuit Intime, The Ball, La Vie des Fantasmes Érotiques et Esthétiques* (balletLORENT).

Opera includes: *The Philosopher's Stone* (Garsington Opera); *Who put Bella in the Wych Elm, Infinito Nero* (Almeida Aldeburgh Opera).

OLLY FOX
COMPOSER

For ETT: *Hamlet* (New Ambassadors), *Twelfth Night, Romeo and Juliet, King Lear* (Old Vic), *The Caretaker, The Taming of the Shrew.*

Other theatre includes: *Ghosts* (The Gate); *Shadowlands* (Salisbury); *Therese Raquin* (National Theatre); *Love And Money* (Young Vic/Royal Exchange); *Much Ado About Nothing* (RSC/ Novello); *A Number* (Crucible/Chichester); *Mary Barton* (Royal Exchange); *Pillars Of The Community* (National Theatre); *Where Do We Live, Mr Kolpert* (Royal Court); *Bones; Hand in Hand* (Hampstead); *Thyestes* (RSC The Other Place); *Gone To Earth* (Shared Experience); *The Cherry Orchard* (Southwark Playhouse); *The Wasp Factory* (Northern Stage); *The Importance Of Being Earnest* (Oxford Playhouse); *The Good Woman of Setzuan* (National Theatre Mobil Tour); *To Kill A Mockingbird, Equus, The Duchess Of Malfi, Macbeth, The Winter's Tale* (Salisbury); *Secret Heart, The Way Of The World, Two Clouds Over Eden* (Royal Exchange); *Things Of Dry Hours* (Royal Exchange/The Gate); *The Three Birds* (The Gate); *News From The Seventh Floor* (Wilson&Wilson/ Watford Palace); *Hospital Works* (theatre-rites/Theater Der Welt, Stuttgart); *The Mill On The*

CREATIVE TEAM BIOGRAPHIES

Floss, A Midsummer Night's Dream (Contact Theatre).

TV includes: *The Life & Times Of Vivienne Vyle* (BBC/Saunders & French); *Timewatch: Inside The Mind Of Hitler* (BBC).

Radio includes: *Tin Man, Alice Through The Looking Glass, Millport* and many other plays for BBC Radio.

MIKE FURNESS
SOUND DESIGNER

Theatre Sound designs include: *A Fine Balance* (Hampstead); *Babe* (Regent's Park); *The Trouble With Asian Men* (Arts Depot); *On Religion* (Soho); *Child of The Divide* (UK & US Tour); *All's Well That Ends Well* and *As You Like It* (RSC); *Blues In The Night, The Witches, Ladyday* and *The BFG* (West End); *Mother Courage* (National Theatre); and shows for The Tricycle, Paines Plough, Theatre Royal Stratford East, Lyric Hammersmith, Birmingham and Leeds Rep, Bristol Old Vic, Brighton &

Edinburgh Festivals.

As well as producing Talking Books he designs sound for a diverse range of live events.

BETHANY ANN McDONALD
ASSISTANT DIRECTOR

Directing credits include: *Desdemona, a play about a handkerchief* (LAMDA); *Sure Thing* and *Words, Words, Words* (LAMDA); *The Lover* (BeesKnees Pros, NYC); *Goober's Descent* (The Atlantic Acting School, NYC); *Cowboy Mouth* (Proud Mother Pros, Athens, Greece).

AD credits include: Moliere's *Don Juan* with Bartlett Sher for Theatre For A New Audience, NYC; *Lemonade* by Eve Ensler with David Wheeler at the Wellfleet Harbor Actors Theatre, Cape Cod, MA; and *Hobson's Choice* with Stephen Jameson at LAMDA.

Bethany is a graduate of the LAMDA Postgraduate Director's Course, 2006, and is a

member of the 2003 Lincoln Centre Theatre Directors' Lab in New York City.

PENNY DYER
DIALECT COACH

Theatre includes: *Frost/Nixon* (Donmar and West End); *There Came a Gypsy Riding, Tom and Viv, The Late Henry Moss, An Earthly Paradise, The Mercy Seat* and *I.D.* (Almeida); *The Winter's Tale, The Crucible* (RSC); *The Cryptogram* and *After Miss Julie* (Donmar); *Fiddler on the Roof* and *Girl in a Goldfish Bowl* (Crucible); *Summer and Smoke* (Nottingham and West End); *Royal Hunt of the Sun* (NT); *Philadelphia Story* (Old Vic); *Down Under* (Tricycle); *The Woman in White, Solid Gold Cadillac, A Woman of No Importance* and *My Fair Lady* (West End); *Electricity* (WYP); *Skellig* (Young Vic); *Happy Days* (Arts).

Television includes: *Fantabuloso, The Deal, Blackpool, Shadow in the North, North and South, Pierrepont, Crocodiles* and *Monsters.*

CREATIVE TEAM BIOGRAPHIES

Film includes: *The Queen, The Golden Age, Infamous, Mrs Ratcliffe's Revolution, Nanny McPhee, The Da Vinci Code, Mrs Henderson Presents, Dirty Pretty Things, On a Clear Day, Ladies in Lavender, The Importance of Being Earnest, The War Zone, Elizabeth.*

Penny is currently working on *King Lear* for the RSC, and *Boeing Boeing* for SFP.

GINNY SCHILLER
CASTING DIRECTOR

For ETT: *The Old Country, Hamlet* (both also West End), *French Without Tears, Mother Courage and Her Children, Rosencrantz & Guildenstern Are Dead, Twelfth Night.*

Theatre includes: the RSC's *Complete Works Festival* and *The Canterbury Tales* (tour and West End transfers); *Macbeth* and *How Many Miles to Basra?* (West Yorkshire Playhouse); *The May Queen* and *All My Sons* (Liverpool Playhouse); *Dr Faustus* and *The Taming of the Shrew* (Bristol Old Vic); *The Importance of Being Earnest* (Oxford Playhouse); *A Passage to India* (Shared Experience); *Macbeth* (Albery); three years as Casting Director for Soho Theatre, three seasons for Chichester Festival Theatre and five years with the RSC.

Television and film includes: *The Kingdom, Notes on a Scandal, The Miracles of Jesus, George Orwell – A Life in Pictures* (Emmy Award Winner), *The Bill, The Falklands Play.*

Radio includes: *The Pickwick Papers, Tender is the Night, The Bride's Chamber.*

RACHEL TACKLEY
PRODUCER

Rachel is a freelance producer and creative producer for ETT. Recent productions include: *French Without Tears* and *Mother Courage* (national tour), *The Old Country* and *Hamlet* (national tour and West End) for ETT; *Yellowman* by Dael Orlandersmith (national tour) with Liverpool Theatres; and Mark Healey's adaptation of Fowles' *French Lieutenant's Woman* (national tour). Rachel has produced numerous shows for Shared Experience Theatre in the UK, USA and all over the world. She is also Chief Executive of Milton Keynes Theatre.

OUR SUPPORTERS

We are indebted to all those who have supported ETT and would like to extend our gratitude to all our supporters.

If you are able to lend your support by making a financial contribution whether through a gift, sponsorship or membership, we would be delighted to discuss the opportunities with you. For further information, please contact our Development Department on 020 7450 1990.

ETT
IGLISH
URING
EATRE

Would you like to keep in touch?

Hamlet, 2005

We hope you enjoyed seeing us on stage.

Would you like us to keep you informed about our future productions? If so, you just need to take a moment to complete an ETT mailing list card which is available front of house and return it to us at the FREEPOST address at no cost to you.

Mother Courage, 2006

Or visit **www.ett.org.uk** and sign-up to our mailing list on-line.

Alternatively you can contact us at:

25 Short Street
London
SE1 8LJ

Rosencrantz and Guildenstern are Dead, 2005

Tel: 020 7450 1990

The Old Country, 2006

www.ett.org.uk
admin@ett.org.uk

Photography by
Stephen Vaughan
and Robert Day

● **soho** theatre

Soho Theatre is passionate in its commitment to new writing, producing a year-round programme of bold, original and accessible new plays – many of them from first-time playwrights.

'a foundry for new talent . . . one of the country's leading producers of new writing'

Evening Standard

Soho Theatre offers an invaluable resource to emerging playwrights. Our training and outreach programme includes the innovative Under 11s scheme, the Young Writers' Group (18-25s) and a burgeoning series of Nuts and Bolts writing workshops designed to equip new writers with the basic tools of playwriting. We offer the nation's only unsolicited script-reading service, reporting on over 2,000 plays per year. We aim to develop and showcase the most promising new work through the national Verity Bargate Award, the Launch Pad scheme and the Writers' Attachment Programme, working to develop writers not just in theatre but also for TV and film.

'a creative hotbed . . . not only the making of theatre but the cradle for new screenplay and television scripts'

The Times

Contemporary, comfortable, air-conditioned and accessible, Soho Theatre is busy from early morning to late at night. Alongside the production of new plays, it is also an intimate venue to see leading national and international comedians in an eclectic programme mixing emerging new talent with established names.

'London's coolest theatre by a mile'

Midweek

●**soho** theatre

The Terrace Bar

The Terrace Bar on the second floor serves a range of soft and alcoholic drinks.

Email information list

For regular programme updates and offers, join our free email information list by emailing box@sohotheatre.com or visiting www.sohotheatre.com/mailing.

Hiring the theatre

Soho Theatre has a range of rooms and spaces for hire. Please contact the theatre managers on 020 7287 5060 or go to www.sohotheatre.com for further details.

Soho Theatre

Soho Theatre, 21 Dean St, London W1D 3NE
Admin: 020 7287 5060 Box Office: 0870 429 6883
Minicom: 020 7478 0136 www.sohotheatre.com
email: box@sohotheatre.com

SOMEONE ELSE'S SHOES

Drew Pautz

.

Characters

JED PILLAR, *a late-twenties ex-student.*

NADINE SANDERSON, *a talented and ambitious multimedia and conceptual artist; Jed's girlfriend.*

ADAM AMEDEO, *an extremely wealthy and influential American art collector and gallery owner; advertising head of the former Amedeo family business, Mercury Shoes, now a subsidiary of a massive multinational corporation.*

RICHARD AMEDEO, *former co-owner of Mercury Shoes, now, after its public sale and takeover, president; Adam's older brother.*

MARY KLEMP, *an activist.*

The action of the play takes place in Rome and Toronto over the course of a few months in the present.

This text went to press before the end of rehearsals so may differ slightly from the play as performed.

Scene One

ADAM *and* NADINE *on cell phones*; NADINE *wears a white T-shirt emblazoned with large black letters:* I'M IN YOUR VIDEO. *The following overlaps where necessary.*

NADINE (*low throughout*). Hello?

ADAM (*low throughout*). Hi, Richard.

NADINE. I knew it'd be you.

ADAM. Calm down, Richard.

NADINE. Jed, that's what I *mean*: 'I hoped.'

ADAM. Italy.

NADINE. What?

ADAM. That's what I said, yes: Italy.

NADINE. No. No. Because I won't.

ADAM. Well, I like Italy, for one –

NADINE. Because I'm in public.

ADAM. It's not a vacation, Richard, I'm thinking.

NADINE. Alright, okay okay, just –

ADAM. No. Nothing's wrong.

NADINE. My Adidas, my Levi's, the video shirt obviously – happy?

ADAM. Not everything happens in an office.

NADINE. You're *what*?

ADAM. Well you can laugh if you want, but, yes, I am in fact talking about inspiration.

NADINE. Jesus, Jed . . .

ADAM. Richard? Are you there?

NADINE. Jed, listen to me – Jed –

ADAM. Richard?

NADINE. Jed, *I'm in the Sistine Chapel.*

> *Little pause.*

ADAM. Sorry, reception in here is shit.

NADINE. Yes really.

ADAM. Look, don't worry.

NADINE. Please, Jed, what do you want?

ADAM. I think we're breaking up – Richard?

NADINE. I thought you were looking for a job.

ADAM. Richard? (*To* NADINE.) Excuse me.

NADINE. You're a full-grown man, Jed. Try something.

ADAM (*to* NADINE). Excuse me. What's your number?

NADINE (*to* ADAM). Sorry?

ADAM. It's an emergency.

NADINE (*to* ADAM). I'm on the phone. (*Phone.*) No. There's . . . this guy.

ADAM. *Please.*

NADINE. I don't know, just some – hold on a second.

> NADINE *and* ADAM *stare at one another.*

> 001 . . . 416 –

ADAM (*overlapping into phone*). 001 416 . . . (*To* NADINE.) Yes?

NADINE. 418 . . . (*Phone.*) Sorry, this is weird.

ADAM (*overlapping*). 418 –

NADINE (*to* ADAM). 3966. (*Phone.*) Of course I do. You're my boyfriend.

ADAM (*overlapping*). 3966. Got that? Call me on that number if we . . . Richard? Damn.

NADINE (*overlapping*). It's nothing, it's just – Look, I have to – I *promise*, okay? I've gotta go, Jed. Bye.

> NADINE *begins to put away her phone.*

ADAM. Don't turn that off.

NADINE. Sorry?

ADAM. Please don't turn that off.

> *Little pause.* NADINE*'s phone rings. She answers, self-conscious . . .*

NADINE. Hello? (*To* ADAM.) Adam . . . ?

ADAM (*taking the phone*). Look, it's under control, Richard, you don't need me there for – I am not raising my voice. No, I know I'm not because I'm in the Sistine Chapel, Richard.

> You fuck off, you should see it . . . Well you should see it again. Listen, someone's waiting for the phone, I'll be there – It's not a holi – Good. Thank you. (*Hangs up.*)

> *He returns the phone to* NADINE.

> If it's any consolation, that was important. In a way.

NADINE. Great.

ADAM. Always seems to interfere, doesn't it? Business.

NADINE. I guess.

ADAM. I'm trying to apologise.

NADINE. I know.

> *As* NADINE *looks to the ceiling* ADAM *looks from the ceiling to Michelangelo's* The Last Judgement *on the altar wall:*

ADAM. The story of life, huh? From beginning to *The Last Judgement*. That's the one I like.

NADINE. One doesn't expect to be hit on in a chapel. Even in Italy . . . Maybe it's ill-considered fraternity because you're American or something, but it's distracting.

ADAM. You're not American?

NADINE. I'm not interested.

ADAM. I like your T-shirt.

NADINE. 'She was asking for it, your honour'?

ADAM (*guessing*). Student? Art historian?

NADINE. *Artist*. And you? Connecting the dots between meetings? Power breakfast, check, Vatican, check, little piece of ass, check . . .

Little awkward pause.

Look. It's fine, sorry. Apology accepted.

ADAM. Would you join me for dinner?

NADINE. I have to get back.

ADAM. Boyfriend. (*She looks confused.*) Phone.

NADINE: Oh. No. Yes, in Toronto, but . . . Work.

ADAM (*overlapping after 'Toronto'*). I have business interests in Toronto.

NADINE. Really?

ADAM. No strings attached. A decent meal on me. You can tell me about your art.

They look at one another a moment.

NADINE. It's not the kind of thing you hang on your wall.

ADAM. My walls are full. My mind's open.

NADINE. That's kind, really, but . . . I can't. Thanks.

ADAM (*handing her a business card*). Well . . . Let me give you one of these anyway . . . before I'm crucified by the Romans here – or you. *Ciao.*

NADINE *examines the card as he turns away.*

NADINE (*shocked*). I . . .

ADAM *stops. Turns back.*

I had no idea.

ADAM. The *Ambasciata d'Abruzzo*, ten p.m. Parioli. I'll be there regardless. If you want to change your mind.

NADINE: Fuck. Sorry.

Yes.

I mean . . . I would.

Scene Two

JED *waits in a simple room in the new offices of Mercury Shoes, Toronto.* RICHARD *enters, reading a CV.*

JED. Oh. You're –

RICHARD. Visiting.

JED. Right.

RICHARD. Fixing someone else's problem. This is amazing.

JED. Thank you, sir.

RICHARD. Really, incredible.

JED. Thank you.

RICHARD. You're unbelievably over-qualified.

JED. Sorry?

RICHARD. Yet it appears you've hardly ever actually worked.

JED. Oh. Well. That's not entirely –

RICHARD. Do you mind taking a step back?

JED (*standing*). Er . . . I'm sorry – if I've wasted your time.

RICHARD. I just wanna get a good look at your tie and your shoes. I'm impressed. You know what they say about shoes – (*Checking CV.*) Jed?

JED. No, I don't think so . . .

RICHARD. I've heard it a million times: 'You can tell everything about a man by his shoes.'

JED. Really?

RICHARD. What do your shoes tell you?

JED. Uh . . . I don't know.

RICHARD. Give it a shot.

JED. Well, they're brogues.

RICHARD. Yes.

JED. I'm dressed up.

RICHARD. You are.

JED. I've made an effort to look . . . professional, because I care about this interview.

RICHARD. You know what you've applied for, Jed?

JED. 'Retail Communications Liaison Sales Partner Representative.'

RICHARD. Retail clerk. In a shoe store.

JED. Right.

RICHARD. Selling running shoes.

JED. Yeah.

RICHARD. I don't think people who apply for this kind of thing wear brogues, and they don't wear ties. They wear metal in their eyebrows and pants that hang below their ass. (*Consulting CV*.) They haven't spent *nine years* in college.

JED. No, I suppose –

RICHARD. Were there any subjects you *didn't* do?

JED. Business.

RICHARD. Nine years to get a BA?

JED. Um . . . I have a doctorate, sir.

RICHARD. Really?

JED. Philosophy. 'Platonic Form and Evolutions of – '

RICHARD. Which you chose to leave off your CV?

JED. I thought it might not be appropriate.

RICHARD (*beat, then*). Tell me, Jed. Why do you want to work here?

JED. Well . . . I've been wearing Mercurys since I was a little kid, and – not only do I love the brand, but it's been a big, big part of my life. So when I heard Mercury was opening a flagship Planet store here in Toronto, I thought, you know, 'You are the message: Mercury.' That was revolutionary, that campaign. It inspired me – it still inspires me, so I guess you could say I've kind of grown up with Mercury all my life, you know. Like a friend.

Pause.

RICHARD. Bullshit.

JED. Sorry?

RICHARD. What you're saying sounds like bullshit.

JED. Actually most of it's from your commercials.

RICHARD. I know where it's from. Coming out of your
mouth it sounds like bullshit. If you'll excuse my French.

JED. I should go.

RICHARD. Sit, Jed. I want to know why you want to work
here. Really.

JED *considers, then* . . .

JED. I don't.

RICHARD. Right.

JED. I mean, I do. I need a job, but . . . Sorry.

RICHARD. Please. I'm fascinated.

JED (*beat, then*). Well . . . I've got a lot of debt.

RICHARD. Okay.

JED. And I guess . . . It's. Well, I understand the exchange of
labour, the importance of a stable economy for healthy society
and everything, but when you're talking about the individual,
about . . . personal desire, I suppose, the concept of employ-
ment's kind of abstract, isn't it? I guess you could talk about
it existentially, or in terms of ethics, but I just mean logic:
'What do you do?' I mean, unless it's a vocation, people who've
always dreamt of being a doctor or a ballet dancer or – but
when push comes to shove, I mean, how do you choose?
You know, what you want to do? But I still need a job.

RICHARD. Everyone needs a job.

JED. You're Richard Amedeo, aren't you?

RICHARD. I'm in Toronto for twenty-four hours, Jed.

JED. Yeah . . .

RICHARD. I'm looking for my brother. I'm not here to do
admin.

JED. No, I didn't think –

RICHARD. They got a hundred and eighty applications out there.

JED. Really?

RICHARD. A hundred and eighty people who *want* to do this job. And you.

JED. Right.

RICHARD. I told them I'd demonstrate how to make a decision in less than five minutes.

JED. Really.

RICHARD. Because it's about application, not *the* application, Jed. You wanna talk personal desire? America's about making something yourself, making something out of yourself –

JED. This is Canada –

RICHARD. Yeah yeah, 'North America,' I know, it's a figure of speech, Jed –

JED. Right.

RICHARD. You can't opt out.

JED. No.

RICHARD. You're either in this world, or you're dead. That's the truth.

JED. Okay . . .

RICHARD. I'm speaking philosophically here, Jed.

JED. I know.

RICHARD. I'm saying people used to work from the bottom up. Not a business concept, simple hard work. Do you think you could do that?

Pause.

You wanna flip a coin, or what?

JED. I really need a job, Mr Amedeo.

RICHARD. Say you want it, Jed.

JED (*beat, then*). I want it.

RICHARD. 'I want it.'

JED. I want it.

RICHARD. 'I want it.'

JED. I want it.

RICHARD. 'I want it.'

JED. I want it.

Little pause.

RICHARD. Good. Now I've got to track down my fuckin' brother.

Scene Three

JED *and* NADINE *in their basement apartment – lived-in, untidy, but not a disaster.* NADINE *has just returned from Italy.*

NADINE. I like what you've done with the place.

JED. You know, bachelor life.

NADINE. I was gone five days.

JED. Eternity. How was it?

NADINE. Okay.

NADINE *begins to unpack.*

JED. I imagine all these video cameras trained on you, at the, at the, the fountain, the whatsit fountain or the Spanish Steps or something. Then, slowly, with each step, you take something off. Shoes, jeans, bra . . . *panties*. Till it's just the T-shirt 'cross your mid-thigh, just, *just* covering . . . And you're eating *gelati*.

NADINE. That's not quite how it happened.

JED (*a sexual approach*). No, but in my version . . .

NADINE. I'm sorry. I can't . . . I'm tired.

JED. No. No, I'm sorry . . . Of course. Sorry. (*Beat, then.*) Can't or won't?

NADINE. Jed, please . . .

JED. I got a job.

NADINE. What?

JED. I thought we might want to celebrate. That's all.

NADINE. A job? That's. Fantastic. Where?

JED. Uh. Well . . . Sales. You know.

NADINE. No.

JED. Selling stuff . . . (*Beat, then.*) Mercury Planet.

NADINE. The shoe store?

JED. It's actually a Sports Entertainment and Community Complex.

NADINE. Oh, *Jed* . . .

JED. The good thing is they don't hire full-time so it allows me time to do other . . . stuff, you know. So . . . (*Beat.*) You wanted me to get a job.

NADINE. What other *stuff* do you do?

JED. What does that mean?

NADINE. Look around, Jed. We live in a basement, we're still crawling round in the muck down here like amoebas or something, and you're standing there waiting all the time like there's ever going to be some big formal invitation. I'm trying so hard.

Pause.

JED. What happened in Italy, Nadine?

NADINE. Nothing. Nothing, I'm tired, I'm sorry. Congratulations on the job. You've made your point, do what you want. Quit, get fired, whatever, I just want to sleep.

JED. I was interviewed by Richard Amedeo, you know.

NADINE. What?

JED. Yeah.

NADINE. Really?

JED. Weird, eh?

NADINE. Yes, very.

JED. It was like meeting Machievelli's archetypal prince or something. He said I was completely over-qualified.

NADINE. Did you tell him you're a doctor?

JED (*small beat, then*). No. I . . . Okay, I'm not going to identify myself on a plane or anything but –

NADINE. You never wrote a thesis.

JED. I had issues with the process. I could have.

NADINE. I can't believe you walk into the first fuckin' store you see for an answer.

JED. To what? Answer to what? I don't know what's going on, but thank you, your faith moves mountains – I applied for this job, I'm trying to make you happy, I'm not going to be fired –

NADINE. Okay.

JED. I'm not.

NADINE. Okay.

JED. I mean, everyone thinks it comes down to . . . you think – just because you've got . . . I don't even know what we're talking about.

Silence.

I love you, Nadine.

NADINE. I love you too.

Pause.

JED. But what?

NADINE. This isn't working.

Scene Four

MARY *in Mercury Planet, the Mecca of sport shoes retailing. She examines a display shoe; an unmarked, bulging duffle bag rests at her feet. JED enters in a Mercury Planet uniform and watches before approaching.*

JED. That's a beautiful shoe.

MARY. It's nice . . .

JED. It's a reissue: the Mercury Messenger.

MARY. Really?

JED. Story is, the seventies, the Amedeo brothers were amazed there was no tennis shoe made with the same rigour as the racquets and stuff. The humble foot ignored. So they dedicated themselves to the sole and . . . of course, they were still made for tennis then, but the same lines: vintage, classic –

MARY. Nostalgic.

JED. Well, yeah . . . Retro, I guess.

MARY. In grade seven my teacher asked us, 'If Mercury is the messenger god of the Romans, does anyone know who's the messenger god of the Greeks?' and I was so proud of my esoteric knowledge I didn't even raise my hand, just blurted out – 'Herpes.'

JED (*beat, then*). Right.

MARY. A hundred and sixty dollars is a lot to pay for a shoe.

JED. Listen, I hate to do this, but . . . I've been watching you. That's why I came over.

MARY. I thought you came over because you're a salesperson and I'm a customer-person.

JED. I've been watching.

MARY. Or maybe you came over to flirt. Fellow-citizen.

JED. I'm going to have to ask to see in your bag.

MARY. Do you honestly believe that stuff about 'masterpiece' and 'classic,' or is that like the same special lexicon as, 'Oh, those look *really* good on you'?

JED. Really. I've seen you.

MARY. You are flirting with me.

JED. You can't sell them, you know. That's why we only put out singles. (*Beat, then.*) May I look in your bag, please?

MARY. I'm not even at the till yet.

JED. I don't think the Geneva Convention or whatever really applies here.

MARY. I chose your section because you're not the type . . . (*Reading badge.*) 'Sheriff Jed.' It shows. I don't think you're experiencing optimum job satisfaction.

JED. Really?

They stare at one another a moment.

MARY. Hermes is the Greek version of Mercury, you know.

JED. Yeah . . . ?

MARY. Or the other way round. Also the god of thieves.

JED. Great.

MARY. Patron of commerce *and* of thieves. Think about that.

JED. Do you want me to explain my problem here?

MARY. This is stage one. Disturbance.

JED. Sorry?

MARY. Why do you have to work here?

JED. Look, I don't want to have to –

MARY. Restrain me and I'll sue. I know my rights.

JED. I'm not touching you.

MARY. I know.

Pause.

JED. My other problem . . . see. There's a shitload of paperwork to bust a shoplifter.

MARY. Activist.

JED. Whatever.

MARY. Labels are important.

JED. Suppose I wasn't looking for a second.

MARY. Are you saying I should run for it?

JED. I'm saying that bag might slow down your escape.

MARY. Ah.

JED. Just . . . (*Demonstrating*.) If I looked down, say, to tie my shoe or something, you know, and I went real slow and you left the bag and the shoes and I looked up and . . .

MARY *and her duffle bag are gone*.

Fuck.

Scene Five

NADINE *in her studio, which is dominated by a large grey filing cabinet*. ADAM *has just arrived*.

NADINE. Oh. Hello.

ADAM. 'Oh. Hello.'

Pause.

NADINE. Sorry. I'm surprised.

ADAM. The door was open. Didn't Jennifer . . . my PA . . . ? She didn't call.

NADINE. Sweet girl, high squeaky voice?

ADAM. That's her.

NADINE. About three minutes ago?

ADAM. Probably. She's in New York. I try to come without fanfare so I can see work *in situ*.

NADINE. That's very superhero-like of you.

ADAM. You're angry.

NADINE. I'm surprised. And I'm a slow learner; so for the moment I'm cautious.

ADAM. I told you we were opening new offices; a new Mercury Planet; new line of shoes. So here I am.

NADINE. On business.

ADAM. It's a nice town.

NADINE. 'Boring.'

ADAM. It's civic. Very clean.

NADINE. 'Thank you,' she said politely.

ADAM. And I'm opening my new gallery, Nadine, which I know you know because I told you. Everyone knows.

Pause.

I'm renting a house. Staying for a while.

Little pause.

I'm looking at new work for the gallery.

NADINE. That's why you're here?

ADAM. Mostly. Can I take off my coat?

NADINE. I don't know what to say.

ADAM. I had a good time in Italy, Nadine.

Pause.

Say anything.

NADINE. You're an asshole.

ADAM. Okay.

NADINE. Italy was weird for me.

ADAM. Alright.

NADINE. You know those moments in life that feel like they fracture something open? For a while you're so sure something's going to happen it's like you start living it. Then it doesn't. Nothing happens. Only it's impossible to climb back in and close the shell 'cause it's been cracked. Do you know what I mean?

ADAM. I said I'd come and have a look, and here I am. I'd like to see the video project. If you'll let me.

Little pause.

NADINE (*indicating the file cabinet*). That's it.

ADAM. This? Really?

They stand a moment, neither moves.

Well. What do you think we should do?

NADINE. I'm not sure. Give me your coat.

Scene Six

Very late the same night. JED at home in his Mercury Planet uniform, stretched out, eyes apparently closed, a book on his chest. NADINE has just come in with a designer shopping bag.

JED. What's that?

NADINE. I thought you were asleep. I don't know what it's called. A thing for keeping shoes on.

JED. Feet? You said no luxuries.

NADINE. The closet's overflowing with piles of my shoes, so . . . I sort of need it.

JED. It's two in the morning, Nadine.

Little pause.

NADINE. Jed. I have to tell you something.

JED. Okay.

Little pause.

NADINE. I . . . um . . .

I sold something today.

JED. Really?

NADINE. Thanks.

JED. No, I'm just . . .

NADINE. People *are* interested, you know.

JED. Okay, great, I'm just surprised.

NADINE. They are. Collectors. Like the new Amedeo Gallery, for example. Collectors. (*Beat, then.*) Like Amedeo . . . Adam Amedeo.

Pause.

JED. Isn't he evil?

NADINE. What?

JED. Isn't he a kind of raving power-mad American conservative poster-boy art-world wannabe?

NADINE. You mean unlike his brother, your boss?

JED. He's not really my boss.

NADINE. He's not 'evil', Jed.

JED. You met him?

NADINE. He bought my work.

JED. He just shows up, you meet him, and he buys your work?

NADINE. Basically, yeah.

JED. You met him before.

NADINE. Once.

JED. When?

NADINE. Recently.

JED. How recently?

NADINE. In-the-recent-past recently, does it matter? I wasn't sure I'd sell.

ADAM. You didn't tell me.

NADINE. He wants to buy everything I've ever done. Ever. Since I started.

JED (*beat, then*). And . . . what did you say?

NADINE. I didn't know what to say. I said I'd think about it.

JED. But you said you sold him something.

NADINE. I sold him the 'I'm in Your Video' project.

JED. How much?

NADINE. Fifteen grand. Probably.

JED. YOU WEREN'T SURE IF YOU'D SELL HIM AN IDEA ABOUT VIDEOING YOURSELF FOR FIFTEEN THOUSAND DOLLARS?!

NADINE (*sharply*). We were in negotiations.

JED. Like what?

NADINE. I don't know, the usual – why don't you get out the polygraph and thumbscrews, what is this?

JED. Well you don't *usually* sell work to celebrity collectors then stay out till two in the morning.

NADINE. I was celebrating!

JED. Without me.

NADINE. Jesus . . .

JED. You could have called.

NADINE. I was excited, I'm sorry.

JED. I was slaving all day *at work* –

NADINE. Gimme a break, Jed.

JED. And you don't even bother to phone me with the good news that we're suddenly rich?!

NADINE. I'm rich, Jed; I'm rich, I'm rich, I'm rich, not us! *I'm rich!*

Silence.

I'm sorry.

JED *stares at her for a long time, then begins to gather articles of clothing, etc. strewn about the apartment. He pushes furniture across the floor.*

What are you doing?

JED. What does it look like?

NADINE. You're not finally cleaning, are you?

JED. I'm leaving.

Pause.

NADINE. Jed. It's two a.m.

JED. *I know.*

NADINE. It's freezing out.

JED. I'm not going out. I'm leaving you, not here. This is my apartment too.

NADINE. Don't be stupid.

JED. I'm not waiting around for . . . (*Indicating an imaginary line down the centre of the room*.) My half, your half; unless you're partial.

NADINE. Come on, this is stupid.

JED. It's symbolic. What do you want?

NADINE. Don't.

JED. I want the magazine rack.

NADINE. I don't want to do this.

JED. I want the bookshelves. Your turn.

NADINE. Sit down, Jed. Please.

JED. I want the salad bowl. I want the coasters.

NADINE. Jed –

JED. And the table. Come on! Come on, it's going fast!

NADINE. *Please* . . .

JED. It's your turn. Come on! Big-ticket items all marked down!

NADINE. Stop! Stop it!

JED. I want the toaster! I want the coffee mugs! I want the bed – !

NADINE. I slept with someone else.

Silence.

JED. Oh.

NADINE. There . . .

I'm sorry.

JED. Yeah. Well.

NADINE. I . . . Jed, it's just. It just . . . happened. It's not you.

JED. *Don't say that*.

NADINE. I feel like . . . Oh God, I'm so sorry. I just wanted . . .

JED. Tonight?

NADINE (*beat, then*). In Italy.

JED. Who?

NADINE. It doesn't matter.

JED. It matters to me.

NADINE. Really, I – I didn't want this. (*Beat, then.*) Please talk to me, Jed.

JED. It was my idea too.

NADINE. What?

JED. I'm just saying. 'I'm in Your Video.' We had sex, *made love* in our case . . . then we lay in bed laughing and talking, remember? It was a post-coital concept.

NADINE. You're pathetic, Jed.

JED (*pulling a blanket to his side of the apartment and laying on the floor beneath it*). I have to work in the morning.

Scene Seven

The same night. ADAM and RICHARD in ADAM's Toronto house. ADAM has just arrived home. RICHARD, still in his coat, sits with the lights off.

ADAM. What are you doing in my house?

RICHARD. What's wrong with New York, Adam? Please tell me.

ADAM. Sitting in the dark.

RICHARD. What are you doing in Toronto?

ADAM. New perspective helps me think.

RICHARD. New York has perspective *and* it's new – it's New York, for Christ sake.

ADAM. Richard –

RICHARD. It also has a whole advertising team paid to help you think.

ADAM. I'm going to give you two minutes.

RICHARD. I just want to know what the fuck is going on, is
that unreasonable? I expect you here for the opening, you're
in Italy. I expect you in the Big Apple, you go to Chicago.
I visit the fuckin' Windy City, *now* you're living here in –
what is this, Boredomville?

ADAM. You have a lot of time on your hands for a company
president.

RICHARD. Please tell me you haven't really rented this place.

ADAM. You may have noticed our new offices here, the new
store –

RICHARD. Your new gallery.

ADAM. You're trespassing, Richard.

RICHARD. How many hours a day would you say you're
putting in on the new campaign? And still struggling.

ADAM. I'm not struggling.

RICHARD. Look. We sold the family business, we *invited* this
goddamn takeover, and why was that, huh? I'll remind you.
Because this is where we always wanted to be.

ADAM. I'm watching the second hand.

RICHARD. Because we now have the resources to push
Mercury Shoes to the very limit *and* retain control as long
as we continue to perform, correct? So. Now you've got the
largest palette you've ever had. You've got a team of people
sitting around sharpening pencils waiting for your next big
idea. But you've also got a board of directors, and you're
making me look like an asshole because we have no
campaign. All I'm asking is you put your mind to the task
and do your fucking job.

ADAM. It's not quite that simple.

RICHARD. Which is exactly what I'm saying. You gotta work.

ADAM. Time's up, Dick.

RICHARD. Let me save you an exploratory journey, little
brother. You think you're gonna do mid-life crises different,

but you don't. You buy a better car, you find some charity –
some *art gallery*, even – you get a new young wife, you
build a solarium on the house, you move, you divorce, you
find yourself staying late at the office all over again and
liking it. Golf one afternoon a week, for fuck's sake. That's
what you need.

ADAM. Turn the lights out before you go to sleep, Dick.

RICHARD. Thanks for the hospitality, but I've got a plane to
catch. And, Adam, if I don't wake up to find you in New
York Monday morning, I'm gonna turn round, strap on my
snowshoes, and come back up here to save you myself.

ADAM. What do you think Mercury Shoes would be without
me, Richard?

RICHARD. Look around, Adam. We're the Amedeo brothers.
Me, you, Mercury Shoes. This is who you are.

Scene Eight

MARY *in Mercury Planet; she stands beside her empty duffle
bag, looking at shoes.* JED *enters carrying a stack of shoeboxes.*

JED. Oh fuck.

MARY. Hey, Jed.

JED. I think you should leave.

MARY. I'm window shopping.

JED. You're on the wrong side of the window.

MARY. Just Browsing Thanks . . . You look like shit.

JED. I paid for those shoes, you know.

MARY. What?

JED. The shoes you 'liberated', I paid for them.

MARY. All of them?

JED. I would have lost my job.

MARY. But, that would cost –

JED. Yeah, well, thank God for credit cards, eh?

MARY. Does this mean they don't know a protest was launched against them?

JED. Do you want to know what happens?

MARY. I'm really sorry, Jed –

JED. First I order up replacement pairs for each of the shoes you ripped off which means my name is now in the computer and printed on all the boxes as salesperson, so I have to account for them, which means I have to take them to a bunch of different cashiers so no one notices I'm suddenly Mercury's best customer. And I have to pay cash. Of course, I don't *have* cash, so I use my credit card to get some from the cash machine – my *new* credit card with the shit APR interest –

MARY. You don't have to do this . . .

JED. Then, instead of setting the shoes aside to take home, I take out the rights and put them out on display. But now I've got all these lefts left over. I can't leave with them, can I, because they check staff when we leave and they're going to wonder why I'm buying, like, fifteen pairs of sneakers, and I don't even have any rights. So I have to rip the boxes to shreds and hide them under all the other garbage so nobody gets suspicious. *But I still have shoes*, the lefts, and I can't put them with *your* lefts in inventory and I can't walk out with them so now I have to throw *them* into the dumpster too – brand new shoes – and I have to pretty much climb into the fucking thing in case someone notices a single shoe sticking out which would mean they'd probably find the others and, I'm guessing, it wouldn't take too long to find me, and then . . . then . . . I'm not going to lose this job.

MARY. This wasn't the intended effect, you know.

JED. Yeah, well, there it is. Newsflash: the world is shit, things don't turn out like you want. *They're just shoes* – why don't you go yell at Parliament if you're so committed to 'doing something'?

MARY. Because that whole process is clearly totally and
utterly ineffective.

JED. Which process? Representative democracy?

MARY. I'm just saying, the real centre of power has shifted.

JED. To a shoe store?

MARY. Maybe we should be voting for the big fat CEOs who
really run things. Or line them up against the wall.

JED. Wow, a real live revolutionary socialist.

MARY. I'm not a Marxist, if that's what you mean.

JED. You don't like Marx?

MARY. Parts.

JED. Which parts?

MARY. The part that's still true.

JED. A Marxist shoplifter.

MARY. I'm an activist.

JED. You're a bit loosey-goosey with definitions, aren't you?

MARY. 'Cause they're so easily hijacked. Like 'left' has
become 'wacko' or 'naive'. I mean, even 'anti-
globalisation' is a kind of media word –

JED (*overlapping*). Look, this is very interesting, but . . .

MARY (*continuing*). – when actually the movement's like
more *pro*-globalisation in terms of free movement of
people, ideas whatever. But it's like suddenly in the age of
the 'War on Terror' even debate about the system's
inappropriate or just 'out of fashion' or something, which
seems pretty damn 'convenient' to me.

JED. Don't you think that's a bit simplistic?

MARY. No – And I think it's kinda '*interesting*' the worldwide
capitalist economy that, yes, *Marx* predicted as a necessary
stage in world revolution is steadily advancing, though –
'shock horror surprise!' – not necessarily in tandem with
universal suffrage or democracy. I mean, China isn't exactly
treating their people like the Swedes now they can buy Big

Macs, are they? And Iraq, for instance, isn't exactly a 'reconstructed' democracy even though Halliburton and Betchel and Enron have made their fortune and come back home – oh, wait, not Enron, they're all in jail, aren't they? And meanwhile our governments are more and more concerned with protecting corporate rights rather than people's –

JED. I'm not saying things are –

MARY. And the *people*, people like us, seem to have somehow bought literally this ridiculous idea that somehow we've like *evolved* like Darwin or something to this, our 'natural outcome', the capitalist free market as humanity's most sensitive, just means of interaction –

JED (*overlapping*). Okay . . .

MARY. Like *this* is all some kind of natural phenomenon. It was made by men, you know, it can be changed by men. And women. They might even want to if you bother to ask them.

Silence.

JED. I make *minimum wage* here.

MARY. Which in itself is pretty frickin' weird.

JED. So, am I going to be lined up against the wall, too?

MARY. I don't know. You're getting re-education. You might make it.

Pause.

JED. I wish the world was different too. I really do.

MARY. I get so angry I could kill someone, you know. I mean. I get enraged, don't you? Don't you feel useless sometimes?

JED. I don't know.

MARY. You paid for the shoes.

JED. My life is falling apart, I have an excuse.

MARY. I can't sleep. But every morning I look at the newspaper and I think, 'Am I really part of this?' I mean, we're told this is what's happening, but is it what *happens*?

Really? (*Beat*.) The world is fucked, Jed. I need them to know I'm out here protesting.

JED. Stealing.

MARY. Please stop paying.

JED. Promise you won't steal from my section.

MARY. I won't get you into trouble.

JED. If I catch you, I'll –

MARY. I don't think you will.

Pause.

JED. I have to get back to work.

MARY. My name's Mary. I thought I'd tell you because I don't have one of those badge thingies. 'Mary.' And it's probably good to know your adversary. (*Beat, then*.) Hi.

Scene Nine

Late at night. NADINE in her studio, editing her work. The large filing cabinet, now with drawers open. The floor is littered with photographs, paper, drawings, notes, etc., as well as packed boxes with more of the same. There are piles of video and tape cassettes, DVDs, CDs, a number of tape recorders and a laptop computer. On two monitors NADINE syncs tape to review an edit point and watch material for notes, which she makes in a small black book. On screen NADINE appears in a cheap cable TV studio in the middle of an interview. She is wearing the I'M IN YOUR VIDEO *T-shirt.*

NADINE (*on screen*). . . . So we started to think, well, what if you could actually *appear* in all these tourists' videos, you know?

INTERVIEWER. Yes. Right.

NADINE. Hundreds of them. Eventually you'd get someone showing a DVD to a friend in Hawaii who'd say, 'Wait, wait go back . . . *I knew it* – that girl is in *my* video, too.' Of course we knew we'd have to do something to be noticeable, wear something, so that was the start: 'I'm in Your Video.' And, well, what interested me from the beginning is it's incontrovertibly true: 'I'm in Your Video.'

INTERVIEWER. But the idea evolved – ?

NADINE. Well, yes. It did, yeah. What I'm attempting to do now is appear in as many places as possible. For instance, I'm going to Italy soon: Rome, Florence, Pisa . . . and I also try to get friends wherever they live or go on vacation to stand in for me, which means my shirt, or the slogan at least, can be in hundreds of videos. And the idea is, it also helps destroy that notion of the one 'genuine genius artist,' because there're all these people helping me and sort of playing me or my idea; but also because every video some tourist shoots is simultaneously an original piece of art and a completely useless copy, so, it's like everyone becomes sort of complicit, sort of witness and collaborator, I guess . . .

JED *enters, unobserved, in his Mercury Planet uniform and stands watching* NADINE, *who is now searching for a particular moment on a Dictaphone.*

And this over here, the filing cabinet, is where I'm trying to record the whole process, everything, from the conception of the idea right through to its execution – audio, video, photographs, hotel receipts, *everything*, so – sort of obsessively collected, and documented and filed, so that's sort of the material 'work' for galleries or shows and things.

NADINE *pauses the video to listen to the Dictaphone – a recording of her and* ADAM *at dinner in Rome. She listens intently.*

(*On tape.*) I have a confession to make.

The noise of NADINE *removing the Dictaphone from her pocket or handbag and placing it on a table; the sound becomes clearer . . .*

NADINE *turns and sees* JED. *They look at one another.*

ADAM (*on tape*). A Dictaphone. You're working.

NADINE. It looks really bad, doesn't it, but I'm having such a good time, really.

ADAM (*laughing*). No, no, it's okay, it's – fantastic, actually.
I love it. I surrender. You got me –

NADINE *switches off the tape*.

JED. Hey.

NADINE. Hi.

Pause.

JED. I didn't want to come, but. I locked myself out of the
apartment.

NADINE. It's one a.m. . . .

JED. Yeah, well, I've been working.

NADINE. Right . . .

JED. I'm working extra inventory shifts to keep up with this –
actually it's a long story, but my debt's sorta worse than it
was before, so. You don't care, do you?

Little pause.

Are you going to tell me who you're fucking?

NADINE. No.

JED. You think I'm a loser, don't you?

NADINE. No.

JED. It was okay when we were neck and neck, when I was a
student, but I lost my way, right?

NADINE. Jed . . .

JED. That's what you think. I can't do anything.

NADINE. I can't wait for ever.

JED. For what?

NADINE. Things change, that's all.

JED. So, sever all ties.

NADINE. Well, we're still living in the same apartment –

JED. Happy days.

NADINE. I'm not actually that happy.

JED. Maybe it's selling everything.

NADINE (*handing him the key*). Rent's due in a week, you know.

JED. I'm not moving out if that's what you mean.

NADINE. I'm just saying –

JED. I can pay rent.

NADINE. Fine.

JED (*the key*). I'll leave it under the mat. Try to be quiet on your way in.

JED exits. NADINE stands a moment, then switches the tape back on.

ADAM (*on tape, as before*). *Still.* Not many artists are so – thorough. Travelling halfway round the world.

NADINE. What about you? What are you doing in Rome?

ADAM. I'm trying to change my life.

NADINE. Really? How do you do that?

ADAM. Buy something usually. (*Little laugh.*) Seriously. I think selling something probably does the same.

NADINE. You think?

ADAM. Like the video piece, maybe.

NADINE. I . . . God. I'm flattered of course, I –

ADAM. Might be good for us both.

NADINE. I'm just not sure I can – I mean the idea. It's kind of an evolving thing . . .

ADAM. I'd have to see it, obviously.

NADINE. How much? No, I'm kidding. I'm kidding, really . . .

ADAM. Enough business. To Rome and to art. To change.

The sound of ADAM switching off the 'record' button; tape hiss continues. NADINE stands in thought.

Scene Ten

RICHARD *and* JED *in a room at the Mercury offices.*

RICHARD. It's good to see you, Jed. You're not nervous?

JED. I thought this was a regular performance review.

RICHARD. I happened to be in town. Thought I'd pop in to see how you're getting on.

JED. I'm working hard.

RICHARD. Great. (*With a file.*) You know these?

JED. No.

RICHARD. Sales records. Very odd.

JED. Really?

RICHARD. Yeah. They're yours.

JED. Oh . . . (*Beat.*) OH NO. I think I can explain –

RICHARD. I had a hunch when I hired you you were, what? A maverick? I was gambling.

JED (*overlapping*). It looks weird, I know, but she kept coming back –

RICHARD (*overlapping*). And it seems I was correct.

JED (*continuing*). I kept paying, which was unwise maybe, but –

RICHARD (*continuing*). Because it appears that *you*, Mr Jed Pillar, have been selling a small shitload of sneakers.

JED (*beat, then*). Sorry?

RICHARD. Okay, you're not clearing the fucking catalogue. But these bursts of activity, for a beginner: they're magnificent.

JED. Really . . . ?

RICHARD. I'm pleased. After all, I chose you, didn't I?

JED. Right.

RICHARD. So what the hell's wrong?

JED. Sorry?

RICHARD. You look like shit. Like you're half-asleep.

JED. Oh, no. No, I'm working an awful lot of shifts.

RICHARD. I don't think you're really cut out for Mercury Planet.

Little pause.

JED. But. You just said –

RICHARD. Jed. In the sixties, seventies, everything was product: just the shoes. The eighties was tits and beaches, nineties location, lifestyle. You know what we've got now?

JED. I'm not sure.

RICHARD. 'Philosophy.' 'You are the message,' that's what we're selling: you.

JED. Right.

RICHARD. My brother was one of the first: Advertise the idea of ourselves. Not the shoes, the symbol.

JED. The thing is, I really need this job right now.

RICHARD. Fuckin' genius, I'm not embarrassed to say it. But I'll be honest with you – for my money, Jed, he tends towards a certain erraticism that can be . . . alarming.

JED. Oh.

RICHARD. For instance, where the fuck has he been?

JED. Uhm . . .

RICHARD. He's supposed to be in New York. I'm in New York, our head office is in New York. I might not understand what the hell he does, but I need to see him doing it.

JED. I'm not sure I understand why you're telling me this.

RICHARD. What's a smart guy like you doing in retail, huh? You should be where we're *really* selling.

JED. Do you mean . . . ? I don't really have any experience in advertising.

RICHARD. You have a doctorate, don't you?

JED. Oh, well, I'm flattered, but actually it's in –

RICHARD. So you've written a fuckin' book, don't be
   flattered, grab *Fortuna* by the tits. Open the goddamned
   door.

JED. I don't know.

RICHARD. This is ridiculous. Why not?

JED. Well . . . what would I do?

RICHARD. You'd make more money. You'd make sure he
   shows up; make sure he's in the office not twaddling about
   his art gallery.

JED. I'd be a PA?

RICHARD. You'd be an *assistant*. Learning at the feet of a
   master.

JED. Doesn't he have a PA?

RICHARD. You wouldn't be a fuckin' PA. Jed. I gotta know
   what my little brother is doing. We're family, and this
   business is – I put my life into this. I watch his back, he
   watches mine, how can you lose interest in that? I gotta
   know what he's doing.

   Little pause.

JED. Um. Thank you, Mr Amedeo –

RICHARD. Richard.

JED. But I don't think I can . . .

RICHARD. What?

JED. Well. If I'm reporting to you, and working for him; it sort
   of sounds . . .

RICHARD. Like what?

JED. Maybe I don't understand.

   Pause.

RICHARD. Let's look at it this way. Say someone was selling
   shoes to himself.

JED. Sorry?

RICHARD. Technically this wouldn't be illegal, would it? Just odd. I'm talking about quite a lot of shoes here.

JED. I don't know . . .

RICHARD. And say he was just throwing them away or something. Again, *bizarre*, but the customer's always right, correct?

JED. I guess . . .

RICHARD. Only most people, say, store managers, Jed, unlike you and me, they are not that keen on the subtleties of psychologically motivated action. They tend towards positions more Manichean, wouldn't you say?

JED. Probably.

RICHARD. So if this fella was still struggling to *pay* for all these shoes, and not only that, say he was also carrying a huge amount of other debt, he might feel he was, like you, in a confusing position, mightn't he? He might also be keen to waive all of that debt in a single go.

JED. Yeah. But.

RICHARD. We're all afraid. We don't know what we want – old, new, safety, risk. Most people just want something they'll be comfortable in and they can trust will look good. 'Cause how much you gonna change a fuckin' shoe, right? Mercury's wing. You can't fuck with it. It is what it is and what it means. I'd do pretty much anything for it. What about you?

Scene Eleven

ADAM *and* NADINE *in the new Toronto Amedeo Gallery.*

NADINE. Wow. It's . . . beautiful. Even empty like this.

ADAM. It not empty, it's waiting. But not for ever.

NADINE. I know.

ADAM. I need you to decide.

NADINE. I will.

ADAM. Go all the way back to the Renaissance: Michelangelo was a multitasking entrepreneur who understood image and value. He wasn't afraid of glory.

NADINE. He was Michelangelo.

ADAM. The garret's a romantic story.

NADINE. It's not the money.

ADAM. What is it then?

NADINE. It's just everything I've ever done in one room seems –

ADAM. Your studio –

NADINE. Displaced. Seems extreme.

ADAM. Recreated. Your studio recreated right here in your own room.

NADINE. Why does it have to be everything?

ADAM. It doesn't 'have' to be everything, but I want to show what I saw.

NADINE. I could loan you some stuff. We could see how it goes.

ADAM. I'm a collector, not a museum. It may seem a small distinction, but it's important. That's what each of my shows say: 'This is what I believe in.' If it's loaned, what does that say about me and the work? About us?

NADINE. 'Us . . . '

ADAM. Nadine. Fifteen years ago my first piece was a Warhol. Then I got a Jackson Pollock and I thought they were really fantastic, you know, and they were, they were good decisions but I may as well have been ordering from an L.L. Bean catalogue, you know? People decide you're hanging dollar bills from your wall. They want to know what you do. Then I go to this tiny show in an old bus station. A group of young artists just out of college, and their work was . . . so rough and so vicious, this stuff no one had ever even seen before, and that moment, the newness was so thrilling, that experience: I bought every stick of it, the whole thing. Of course, now those guys, you know who I mean . . .

I can never be an artist, that's not who I am. But I can be context, Nadine – and isn't that what culture is? Things coming together at a certain moment, a time, a place. That's why one piece is – of course it's incredible, it can be amazing – but *this is what I do*, Nadine. Better than anyone else. I find the unknown, find the public and lead them to each other. So when I saw you in Italy, you and the shirt, I was intrigued; but when I saw your studio . . . Because it never fails – when you see all of it, get as much as you can in front of you, it starts to make sense. That's the clay. I want to show your work the way I first saw it.

NADINE (*beat*). I have some conditions.

ADAM. You want to haggle.

NADINE. I don't want people wearing shoes.

ADAM. This is a gallery, Nadine.

NADINE. I want people to understand they're stepping into something. And at the end you emerge into that final room there like this one now – absolutely nothing in it so you can look back here properly. Watch other people engage with the work.

ADAM. I've just given you a whole room to yourself.

NADINE. It's important, Adam, really. You can't be in it and look at it at the same time.

ADAM. We have fifteen other artists. The final room's where we sell catalogues and prints for the whole gallery.

NADINE. It's what my work's about. Please. I want people to see it's interaction with the work that makes it. And keeps it going. That's all I want. Otherwise, it's yours.

ADAM *looks at her. Finally he approaches, removes her shoes, then removes his own. He takes them to the centre of the room, places them side by side as though they were standing on a ledge, and steps back.*

ADAM. The Artist and the Collector. On the brink of success.

Scene Twelve

A dark corridor and a large storage cupboard at Mercury Planet.

JED (*offstage*). Mary, where'd you go?

MARY (*entering*). Over here.

JED (*entering*). This is stupid . . . We can talk out here.

MARY. Hurry up. There are no cameras in here.

> *She yanks him into the cupboard and switches on the light.*
> *She is wearing a Mercury Planet uniform.* JED *wears a*
> *dark suit. They look at one another. Silence.*

JED. What?

MARY. Nice suit.

JED. Thanks.

MARY. I was afraid you got fired.

JED. I got promoted.

MARY. I figured that.

JED. Apparently my sales figures were startling.

MARY. Well. Congratulations.

JED (*her uniform*). Why are you wearing that?

MARY. Were you trying to help me, Jed?

JED. You don't actually work here now?

MARY. You left a gap in the market. I'm infiltrating.

JED. Oh God . . .

MARY. You're going to be a hard act to follow, though.

JED. I'm sure you'll shift your share of prod –

> *She kisses him.*

  Oh . . .

MARY. I'm sorry if I made your life difficult.

JED. Mary . . .

MARY. Shhh . . .

JED. This is . . .

MARY. I'm so excited.

JED. What do you mean, there aren't any cameras – ?

MARY (*overlapping*). I had to see if you were okay.

JED. Okay?

MARY. This is the next stage.

JED. Getting a job?

MARY. Disruption and surveillance. We're stepping things up.

JED. We?

MARY. The cell.

JED. Cell?

MARY. It's kinda like a sleeper cell . . .

JED. See, 'sleeper cell' sounds bad –

MARY (*beginning to undress* JED). I can't believe I'm doing this.

JED. This is my first day. I'm supposed to be on lunch . . .

MARY. I never imagined a necktie involved in foreplay.

JED. Wait, Mary – what the hell are we doing here?

MARY. This doesn't excite you?

JED. I don't know, but . . . I wonder if we should talk about . . . I mean, ethically, things are kind of, well, they're getting pretty . . . complicated.

MARY. We can talk afterwards. I fantasised about this from the first day I saw you.

JED. Mary, I . . .

She drops her shirt.

Oh Jesus.

Scene Thirteen

ADAM *and* NADINE *at* ADAM'*s house*. RICHARD *enters in a winter coat*.

RICHARD. I know it's late, I'm sorry. Fuckin' weather in this country. Hope it's okay I brought a friend . . .

JED *enters behind him*. *Seeing* NADINE.

Oh. Who's this?

ADAM. This is Nadine Sanderson, Richard. She's an artist.

RICHARD. I thought you'd be alone.

ADAM. No.

RICHARD. Well. I'm intruding. Shit. Sorry. But I wanted you to meet Jed Pillar. He's really enjoying working for you, Adam, only he's never actually *seen you*.

ADAM. Hi, Jed.

JED. Mr Amedeo.

ADAM. Adam.

RICHARD. Hiya, Nadine. I'm Adam's big brother.

NADINE. Hi.

RICHARD (*introducing* JED *to* NADINE). This is Jed. Nice place, huh, Jed?

JED. Yes.

RICHARD. Adam doesn't like hotels. Anyway. I wanted you two to break bread before the myth scared him to shit, Adam.

ADAM. It's late.

RICHARD. And I've got a flight to Jersey in three hours, so I brought the latest projections we can look over while we eat.

ADAM. What does Jed do, Richard?

RICHARD. Jed reminds me of you, Adam.

ADAM. Fantastic.

RICHARD. He was a salesman, but he's too good for that.

ADAM. What's he do for me?

RICHARD. Well, pretty much anything. Organise, mind the
    fort –

ADAM. I have a PA.

RICHARD. *Assistant*, Adam . . .

ADAM. Now isn't really a good time to talk.

RICHARD. Do you know, when Adam started working with
    us my colleagues didn't want him? Every inch the playboy.
    I saw the potential.

ADAM. Richard . . .

RICHARD. He knew nothing about advertising then – about
    anything. Just instinct.

NADINE. He's done well.

RICHARD. Of course, Jed has a doctorate.

ADAM. Is that right?

NADINE (*simultaneously*). Really?

RICHARD. Adam never finished school.

ADAM. We're lucky Richard spent so many years studying the
    calculator.

RICHARD (*little laugh*). No, no, hey, don't get me wrong:
    he's an autodidact. I studied, Adam *learned*.

ADAM. Richard . . .

RICHARD. He can tell you what people want before they
    know it themselves.

ADAM. Shall we look at those files in the kitchen, Richard?
    Nadine, why don't you tell Jed about the show? We'll just
    be a moment. Excuse us.

RICHARD. I'll be right back, Jed.

    ADAM *and* RICHARD *exit. Silence.*

JED. *I can't believe this . . .*

NADINE. Jed . . .

JED. I can't believe I didn't figure this out . . .

NADINE. I didn't think . . .

JED. I'm going to be sick.

NADINE. You didn't tell me you'd be working for Adam . . .

JED. Do you always come to his meetings?

NADINE. What are you doing here?

JED. Does he fill you like a roll of bills, Nadine? Shoot his
    load in a wad of fifties?

NADINE. Jesus –

JED. Does he spell 'cunt' with a 'k' when he's counting them
    in their thousands?

NADINE. You are plagued with a total lack of imagination.

JED. I guess we won't be splitting a cab home.

NADINE. It's none of your business.

JED. Don't worry. I'm not interested.

    Pause.

    I can't believe you're fucking *Amedeo*!

NADINE. So are you apparently.

JED. I GOT A JOB, WHAT DO YOU WANT ME TO DO?

NADINE. You're a secretary.

JED. I'm not a – I'm an assistant. Oh God, this is going to
    haunt me. You and Mr Medici romping away in a room of
    wet clay or something.

NADINE. Maybe you need to find someone else, too.

JED. I've got someone else, thank you. She's a twenty-four-
    year-old revolutionary, and she fucks like a rabbit. We do
    things I only ever read about before.

    Pause.

NADINE. This isn't healthy. You have to move out, Jed.

JED. You've got impeccable timing, you know.

NADINE. He loves me.

JED. Oh Christ . . .

NADINE. At least *we get on*.

JED. He's a – he's a player – everyone knows that!

NADINE. Nice suit.

JED. And you? Do you love him?

No answer. Unseen, ADAM enters with brandy glasses and a bottle.

At least I don't have to lie down for it.

NADINE. Fuck you, Jed.

ADAM. Excuse me.

NADINE. Oh . . .

JED. Oh shit.

ADAM. My brother's anxious to show you his favourite paintings of mine, Nadine. The ones that look like something. Maybe Jed and I can chat a little business after all.

NADINE. Right . . . Okay . . . Okay.

NADINE exits. Silence.

ADAM. Brandy?

JED. I don't think so.

ADAM. I'm just doing the math myself. I didn't realise. (*Beat.*) Dick is inherently conservative, Jed. He's afraid of change; but adaptability's what separates us from the other animals, isn't it?

JED. I think I should go.

ADAM. But he isn't stupid. He must see something to take you on. And we do share something, don't we?

JED (*going to leave*). Jesus, okay . . .

ADAM. She's a big girl, Jed; she can make her own choices, right? It's not really about you and me . . .

Pause.

Advertising is shit. I know the world is shit but advertising really is. Maybe I'm jaded.

Little pause.

I'm still looking for ideas, though. Always. (*Beat.*) Like I was looking for Nadine. (*Little laugh.*) You probably think I'm ridiculous, but – Maybe we all need this, something that makes us brave, that might push us. What if I gave you a chance?

Little pause.

Three weeks. Three weeks to figure out what's what and come up with the idea for a campaign that blows the competition out of the water. But it has to be fantastic, or nothing. 'Can't Beat Mercury' is the slogan. Bring me the idea. Push me.

RICHARD *and* NADINE *enter.*

RICHARD. Have you been painting me as some kind of philistine, Adam?

NADINE. He likes the abstract expressionists.

ADAM. Richard'll say anything to please.

RICHARD. Where're you going, Jed?

ADAM. I don't think he's going anywhere, Richard. I just offered him the chance of a lifetime.

Little pause.

RICHARD. And what did he say?

ADAM. I don't think he's made his mind up yet. Have you, Jed?

JED *looks to* ADAM, RICHARD, NADINE . . .

JED. I'm thinking.

Scene Fourteen

JED *and* MARY *in darkness.*

JED (*quietly*). No . . . no . . . no . . . Oh God! No . . . Oh. No.
No no no . . . yes . . . NO!!

(*Calmer; post-coital.*) Oh . . . Jesus.

Silence.

Um . . . We can't keep doing this.

MARY *turns on the light: the cupboard at Mercury Planet.*

MARY. What?

JED. I'm sorry.

MARY. Cupboard sex?

JED. I don't think it's . . . appropriate.

MARY. I think you need to relax.

JED. I have a position to maintain.

MARY. You're a secretary, Jed.

JED. I'm not a secretary.

MARY. Okay, 'assistant', whatever.

JED. I'm not a secretary.

MARY. I don't think they really care about the PA's romantic
life . . .

JED. I was promoted.

MARY. I know, but –

JED. No I mean, again. I'm . . . it's sort of complicated, but.
I'm kinda working in . . . advertising now. I think. (*Beat.*)
I'm under a lot of scrutiny.

MARY *shakes her head in disbelief.*

What?

She lights a cigarette.

Oh, uh . . . I don't think you should smoke.

MARY. Oh Christ.

JED. No it's just, I don't care – but the fire alarms, and . . . (*He coughs.*)

MARY (*putting out her cigarette*). You're asthmatic.

JED. You think I'm a wimp or something because I have asthma?

MARY. I think you're a bit . . . 'something.' Like paranoid schizophrenic.

JED. You never smoked before.

MARY. You weren't trying to dump me before. How does a guy go from being a 'student of thought' or whatever to, like, establishment stooge in six weeks?

JED. I'm not . . . That's not fair.

MARY. *Advertising?*

JED. I've been to some marches and things in my time, you know.

MARY. Yeah, I know, you've told me.

JED. *You* go to marches.

MARY. Marches are advertising.

JED. You steal shoes.

MARY. I *used* to steal shoes.

JED. And now? You're 'infiltrating,' which means . . . ?

No answer.

See? That's what I mean, I'm not good enough for you –

MARY. You are good –

JED. No, you think everything I do is a joke. I'm a challenge, but you don't accept I might be under a lot of genuine pressure, and . . . Look, you're down here doing, I don't know what, I'm up in the office and there's a lot of expectation, and – I'm trying really hard but, well . . . what do you want me to do? March? Donate money? Quit my job? Rid myself of all possessions? I'm not justifying it, I'm just saying I have to do this right now, 'cause it's what

I've got and, I mean, maybe I'll even be good at this, I don't
know, because, well – I'm a little bit older than you, and
I have to get on in this world 'cause it's where I live, and
I'd really love to join another world but I just don't see it . . .
I just . . . I don't. I'm sorry.

Pause.

MARY. Look at you. In knots. You are good. That's why I
chose you.

JED. You didn't choose me.

MARY. You know this thing you call shoplifting.

JED. I don't call it shoplifting, it is shoplifting.

MARY. First time I took something, I was probably, like, nine –
make-up, which is typical, I know, but I was nine. Then
clothes, CDs, then just anything, 'cause I lived in the
suburbs so you go to the mall. And when you go to the mall
you can't come back empty-handed.

JED. Kids steal stuff.

MARY. I didn't choose to take those things, you know. I was
forced. By people like you.

JED. Oh come on –

MARY. And you know what happened every time, afterwards,
what happened when I found myself out there on the
sidewalk again with that duffle bag full of shoes? I cried.
Every single time.

JED. Mary, please understand.

MARY. Every guy I've been with has left me. I scare them.

JED. You don't scare me, Mary.

MARY. It's okay, I understand. Everyone wants guarantees:
what you're going to look like, what you're going to do,
and I can't give that. But what you get will be honest.
People are constitutionally incapable of commitment, aren't
they?

JED. You mean me.

MARY. 'You can't react to every single slight, it's impossible, you'd always be reacting,' that's what we say, right? But why not? Isn't that actually integrity?

JED. Probably. But it's also crazy.

MARY. I don't think you're a joke, Jed. I think you're unhappy and kind of un-self-actualised or whatever. But you want to do something. I want to do something. We can help each other.

JED. But you can't even tell me with what.

MARY. Something big that can carry us both. Help has to be selfless, don't you think? It can't be easy.

JED. Tough love.

MARY. I don't know. Everything effective has to be sorta savage, doesn't it?

JED. I'd like to help *you*, Mary. Really. I would.

MARY. So stay, for a start.

Pause.

Can you hear that?

JED. What?

MARY. The city, Jed. Waking up.

JED. Oh no. Oh, shit shit! What time is it?

MARY. Jed . . .

JED (*frantically gathering his clothes*). Fuck. I have to go . . . Seriously, I have a meeting this morning . . .

MARY. You have to come back tonight, you have to.

JED. I'll try.

MARY. No! That's not enough!

JED (*distracted; dressing*). I've gotta get cleaned up – where's my – ?

MARY (*helping him*). Please.

JED. Thanks.

Suddenly they kiss. It becomes surprisingly passionate.
Then stops.

MARY. I can still taste your doubt.

JED. I have a nine o'clock meeting.

MARY. Promise.

JED. This is completely insane.

MARY. It's shock therapy. Tough, savage cupboard love. It's
what we need.

Scene Fifteen

Very early morning. ADAM at home. He has been working all
night and sits with coffee and his files. NADINE has just
arrived. She's dressed for a party, holding her shoes.

NADINE. We had an agreement.

ADAM. Nadine . . .

NADINE. I thought we agreed.

ADAM. You didn't hurt yourself?

NADINE. No, I didn't 'hurt myself', I was drunk.

ADAM. Yes, I heard.

NADINE. I wanted people to take off their shoes.

ADAM. They saved most of the stuff you threw in the street.
The catalogues, prints . . .

NADINE. I was angry.

ADAM. I'm thrilled. 'No such thing as bad publicity.'

NADINE. I thought that room was going to be empty.

ADAM. Are you okay?

NADINE. *Where were you?*

ADAM. I get in the way of the art, Nadine.

NADINE. It was a private view, no one was looking at the art.
Maybe the art gets in the way of you.

ADAM. In the end it wasn't practical, you understand that, right? Having the final room as your own viewing gallery, taking off shoes. It made you look favoured.

NADINE. You went to another show.

Little pause.

ADAM. Yes.

NADINE. I don't understand –

ADAM. I never go to openings, you know that.

NADINE. I didn't know 'never', no.

ADAM. The event doesn't need me. I always go out and look at new work.

NADINE. You're working on a new show?

ADAM. Nadine. You went. You wore the dress. You threw the stuff into the street.

NADINE. I thought you'd make an exception for me.

ADAM. I am. Please.

Little pause.

NADINE (*a stain on her dress*). I don't even know where this came from.

ADAM. There's always blood the first time.

NADINE *freezes. A long pause.*

NADINE. That's terrible.

ADAM. I came back here and worked on this campaign all night because I have to. There are lots of things we don't want to do but we have to.

NADINE. You're right, you know – it *is* like the first time you fuck: I'm tingling and disappointed and I already want to do it again.

ADAM. Sometimes we just have to compromise.

NADINE. I loved it, Adam. I loved it and I hated it and I was furious but the whole night I felt like it had nothing to do with me any more. Sometime I'd like to just slow down and hold on to something longer than an instant. Can you understand that?

ADAM. I think so.

NADINE. And do you ever feel that? Are you ever certain about anything?

ADAM. All the time.

Little pause. They look at one another.

NADINE. I don't even have a studio now.

ADAM. You still have a studio.

NADINE. I have an empty room and absolutely no idea what I'm doing next.

ADAM. I'd love the chance to start from a clean slate.

NADINE. The grass is always greener, eh?

ADAM. Yes, but sometimes the grass really *is* greener. You should be thrilled this morning, Nadine. It's going to be a huge success.

Little pause. They look at one another.

I wish I did go last night, you know. Honestly. Fuck tradition. Next time I will. Just to see you.

NADINE. I don't have anything to show next time.

ADAM. You'll make something new soon, Nadine. I know you will.

Scene Sixteen

RICHARD *and* JED *in a coffee franchise in Mercury Planet.*

RICHARD. These are great, huh?

JED. Yeah.

RICHARD. The in-shop-coffee-stop. (*The coffee cups.*) Fucking gigantic.

JED. Yeah.

RICHARD. So. What the hell's happened, Jed?

JED. I don't know, I didn't do anything.

RICHARD. Adam just gives you an assignment?

JED. He said he wanted to give me a chance. That's it.

RICHARD. How's he seem? Distracted?

JED. I really don't see him . . .

RICHARD. Fuckin' gallery, huh. Have you seen it?

JED. No.

RICHARD. Worst thing is, I hear it's a bit of a hit. And that
artist he's with – got the fuckin' eye, doesn't he . . .

JED. He wants me to present a campaign, Mr Amedeo.

RICHARD. What? What campaign? Not *the* campaign?

JED. I don't know. Just ideas.

RICHARD. Yeah, of course ideas, *ideas*, but . . . So?

JED. Well, I just started.

RICHARD. Okay, okay, that's fine, that's alright, we'll think of
something.

JED. 'Can't Beat Mercury.'

RICHARD. What?

JED. That's the slogan he's given me. To work with.

RICHARD (*getting out a pen, writing*). 'Can't. Beat. Mercury.'
Okay. Good. By when, when do you have to give him your
ideas?

JED. Next Thursday.

RICHARD. THURSDAY?!

JED. Yeah.

RICHARD. Why didn't you . . . Jesus fuck. Okay. Okay,
'Can't Beat Mercury' . . .

JED. It sounds a bit 'old skool' to me.

RICHARD. Yeah? Good. (*Writing.*) Seventies or something.
Everyone's doing the seventies now, aren't they? Everyone's
always doing the seventies.

JED. Do you know, coffee beans, the coffee bean market is one of the most volatile and harsh cash crops around. For those who actually grow it.

RICHARD (*beat, then*). What?

JED. Coffee. The prices are driven so low by big manufacturers the small growers, peasants, often they can't even survive. Say in Colombia. They end up growing their plants for cocaine production or something. Or starving.

RICHARD. Really . . .

JED. Yeah. But some places sell fair-trade beans, or coffees made with them.

RICHARD. Here?

JED. No.

RICHARD. Right. But you think – what? – we should. These special beans?

JED. I don't know. Maybe.

RICHARD. Coffee isn't really Mercury's thing, you know. This is a franchise.

JED. Yeah. Sorry. I was just commenting.

RICHARD. No. No, *thinking*. That's good, ideas. Don't apologise. Okay. Tomorrow night before I go we gotta meet at my hotel about this thing. So pack your thinking cap, Jedo . . .

JED. Er . . .

RICHARD. What?

JED. I'm sorry. I have an appointment tomorrow.

RICHARD. What – business, social, what?

JED. Well . . . social I guess.

RICHARD. Jed. We've been outflanked and you didn't even fuckin' mention it. But fuck it – fuck it, that's okay, all we can do now is step up and play ball. But you gotta do this, you gotta stay with the game a hundred and ten per cent, you understand? So cancel your 'social appointment'. This is the real thing. (*Beat, then.*) I've heard of fair-trade beans before.

Scene Seventeen

Day. MARY *at work, in her uniform, and* JED *in his suit outside the Mercury Shoes cupboard.*

JED. Can you help me, ma'am?

MARY. What are you doing down here? It's the middle of the day.

JED. I just wanted to talk to you.

MARY. Now?

JED (*beat, then*). I've been thinking. Looking on the internet and – (*Producing some papers.*) Do you know these . . . ?

MARY. Oh, Jed. You're very cute sometimes . . .

JED (*continuing*). Of course you do, but this is the WJM, which is the 'World Justice Movement'; this is 'Global Act' which is – is this awful?

MARY. No.

JED. And I was thinking, that – *I* think you'd be perfect working for one of these: young, smart, committed, sexy as fuck – you'd feel good about yourself –

MARY. How would you feel about yourself?

JED. Mary.

MARY. Better?

JED. So why don't you tell me what you're doing down here?

MARY. What are you doing up there?

JED. I can't come tonight.

MARY. What?

JED. I have a meeting.

Silence.

MARY. Oh.

JED. That's what I wanted to tell you. Sorry.

MARY. Okay.

MARY begins to take off her shoes, unbutton her shirt . . .

JED. What are you doing?

MARY. We can do it now, then. See things through.

JED. Mary . . .

MARY. Fuck. I'm an anarchist I'm a revolutionary I'm an anti-capitalist.

JED. Mary, stop it . . .

NADINE. I'm an anti-monopolist anti-currency-speculationist.

JED. Please stop it, Mary, come on, please. Stop!

He tries to 'shield' her from CCTV cameras, potential staff, etc. . . .

MARY. A good-fuck reprobate degenerate activist but who are you? WHO ARE YOU, WHO ARE YOU, JED, WHO THE HELL ARE YOU REALLY?!

JED. OKAY ALRIGHT, I'LL CANCEL THE FUCKING MEETING! I'LL CANCEL! Put your clothes on for God's sake, someone will see you!

She begins to button up while JED straightens things.

Jesus Christ . . . Are you crazy?

MARY. I need you.

JED. What is your problem, Mary?

MARY. You don't listen.

JED. Okay. My ears are wide open. You want my help? Tell me, now – what you're doing here. I'll help you. I want to help. Ask me now outright what you want me to do. Please . . .

Pause.

MARY. No one's ever tried so hard for me before.

JED. I'm going crazy.

Pause. MARY *leads* JED *into the cupboard, kisses him, then . . .*

MARY. Okay. The first thing to remember is that even theft is part of the system. It's calculated into their costs.

JED. Okay . . .

MARY. They *expect* people to steal. So we were going to have to lift an awful lot of shoes to even be noticed.

JED. So who is 'we'?

MARY. Identities are kept secret. Internet names.

JED. It's a chatroom?

MARY. No, of course it's not, it's a loose affiliation . . .

JED. Of people chatting. On the internet.

MARY. The idea is individuals everywhere can carry out their own attacks and stuff.

JED. 'Attacks'?

MARY. Protests. The next stage was to try to make, like, effigies – fat-cat businessmen outta shoes but with the soles torn off. You know, like a business dummy with no sole.

JED (*overlapping*). I get it. Why did you say 'attacks'?

MARY. To be used at demonstrations, then as installations or whatever at the stores they came from.

JED. So that's what you want to do? Deliver some kind of Trojan Horse?

MARY. Well, the idea kinda evolved.

JED. Right.

MARY. These companies have incredible resources, you know. I mean, nothing we did even made like a dent in the armour. So we decided . . . what if we replaced the soles with plastic explosives?

JED. What?

MARY. Like we could deconstruct the actual product, the labour, resources, whatever went into these shoes and then kind of reconfigure them as dangerous new sneakers.

JED. Symbolically –

MARY. That's where some of them started to get nervous.

JED. Right . . .

MARY. The thing is, nothing was happening. No one even
    notices protest – 'protest what?' So I thought maybe if we
    take these big effigies apart and put some of these new
    sneakers with the plastic explosives back in their original
    boxes, we could reintroduce them into the system.

JED. Reintroduce them . . . ?

MARY. As a kind of sleeping threat. But no one ever did it.
    Things went totally dead.

JED. Well . . . I guess it is difficult to get explosives . . . for
    one thing . . .

MARY. I got some.

    Pause.

JED. Really?

MARY. Yes.

    Little pause.

JED. And you want to . . . What do you want to do? Try . . .
    making these shoes? The threat.

MARY. No. I want to try the explosives.

    Pause.

JED. Mary.

MARY. Listen carefully, Jed.

JED. Mary . . .

MARY. I want you to concentrate.

JED. You're talking about blowing up a building.

MARY. I'm talking about challenging symbols and systems.

JED. There's a whole office block above this store.

MARY. I know.

JED. I mean, we're . . . people work in here.

MARY. Yes, and we work here, so you can get upstairs to make sure –

JED. No, no. NO WAY. This is terrorism.

MARY. Don't say that. No one is going to get hurt, it's not! Economics is war, Jed.

JED. Oh fuck off.

MARY. Everything else is business as usual. *This* is crossing the threshold, actually doing something you can't take back.

JED. No.

MARY. Slow peaceful change is always the placebo, Jed. It doesn't work.

JED. Gandhi? The Velvet Revolution, the Orange Revolution?

MARY. Tiananmen Square.

JED. Martin Luther King.

MARY. 'Cause that race problem just disappeared.

JED. Jesus, Mary . . .

MARY. You think things are slowly getting better?

JED. But things *are* better, I mean for – for millions of people things *are* getting better.

MARY. Relatively speaking, but what does that mean?

JED. Listen to yourself.

MARY. Violence is the currency of the media, Jed. They sniff it out, it's what people understand.

JED. But who do you think does these things, Mary? Fanatics, Mary, lunatics.

MARY. This is what works.

JED. No.

MARY. It is. I'm sorry it's disturbing, but look around. Because you're right. Who's on the front page now? We got out-manoeuvred, we dropped the ball.

JED. What do you think letting off a bomb here's actually going to do?

MARY. It won't be ignored. It might not change the world in one go, but it's like a vow. Hope.

JED. It's nihilism!

MARY. No, it's not. This says, I believe there's another possibility, I believe it so much, so much, Jed, I am willing to do this, and I have to be taken seriously. You'll be able to shed all this. And no matter what happens, it'll be ours.

JED. I've got to go back up there.

MARY. Kiss me. Please.

JED. I can't.

MARY. Look at you. You have a job you didn't want and don't like, an apartment you can't really use, you're dragged into a cupboard every single night for sex with a woman you don't even trust. You're a walking billboard for equivocation, Jed. I'm making it easy for you. One decision at a time. Be here Thursday night. Wear something black. Everything can still change.

Scene Eighteen

Night. NADINE *and* ADAM *are sharing a table at an upscale skyscraper restaurant.*

ADAM. I've been giving this a lot of thought. I'm not saying I can fix things, but I want to give you something. (*Reaching into his pocket.*) Before you jump to conclusions . . .

NADINE. I'm not jumping. Yet.

ADAM. That's not funny.

NADINE (*the envelope*). What's this?

ADAM. Open it.

NADINE. A cheque?

ADAM. To help you work in peace.

NADINE. What do you get?

ADAM. I thought you might be pleased.

NADINE. You own my ideas?

ADAM. Of course not.

NADINE. The gangster's moll . . .

ADAM. Oh, stop it, Nadine! I want to give you the opportunity to work with some independence – which I can actually *do*.

NADINE. This is your idea of independence? Charity?

ADAM. Possibility. You can buy yourself some time.

NADINE. But I've got loads of time.

ADAM. Or whatever else.

NADINE. What are you asking me, Adam?

ADAM. I'm giving you something.

NADINE. A piece of paper.

Pause.

ADAM. I've got this place in Colorado surrounded by forty acres of pine, Nadine. And there's this little brook runs right under the balcony you can hear all night. It's a babbling brook, literally. And when you sit there for a while it's like the rest of the world sort of fades away. I've always dreamt of moving there someday, concentrating on what I do but slowing down. I want to put a studio on that house. I want you to be able to create whatever you want to your heart's content. Or not.

Pause.

NADINE. Are you saying I could do whatever I want and you'll finance it?

ADAM. More or less.

NADINE. How will I know if it's any good?

ADAM. Sorry?

NADINE. If I never sell anything? How will I know it's any good?

ADAM. You can still sell stuff. What we don't want to keep.

Little pause.

NADINE. Move in with me.

ADAM. Pardon?

NADINE. Move in with me. Into my place.

ADAM. We've never even been to your place. You said it's a
    shithole.

NADINE. It's a basement, but the rent's cheap.

ADAM. Nadine . . .

NADINE. We can split it.

ADAM. I can't move into your apartment, Nadine.

NADINE. But you've got loads of extra money you can give
    away, don't you?

Pause.

ADAM. Why are you sabotaging this?

NADINE. I don't know.

Pause.

ADAM. I'm going to leave the business, Nadine.

NADINE. I thought your business was started by your family.
    I thought you invented the shoes.

ADAM. You don't know anything about business.

NADINE. But you're a businessman. How are you going to
    support the galleries? I thought you sold shoes.

ADAM. No, I collect art, Nadine, I am an art collector. I thought
    I made that perfectly clear. I collect art, that's what I do.
    Sitting right in front of you right here, this is me. Right
    here. Me.

Silence. ADAM *retrieves the envelope and puts it away.*

I don't care if you're making new work or not. Don't say
anything.

Scene Nineteen

ADAM, RICHARD *and* JED *around a boardroom table*. JED *is visibly disturbed. Beside* ADAM, *again, his files.* ADAM *and* RICHARD *stare at* JED.

JED. Well. Uh . . . I found it kinda hard, actually. I really only have one idea. It's . . . kind of a disease campaign, I guess.

RICHARD. Disease?

ADAM. Richard . . .

RICHARD. What disease? I thought it was 'old skool'?

JED. Well, it could be almost any disease, but . . . the first one might be herpes.

RICHARD. Herpes – the venereal disease herpes?

JED. Yeah . . .

RICHARD. Oh my God . . .

JED. See, um . . . I thought . . . You start with old photos and diagrams. When herpes was really, bad, you know. Close-up warts, medical photos, that sort of thing. That's all people see, like, 'What's this?' There's no text.

RICHARD *looks horrified;* ADAM *leans forward, intrigued*.

And uh. Then, next stage, we show people suffering from herpes, people now, guys with sores on their mouths in doctors' offices, women at their gynaecologist's.

RICHARD. I don't believe this.

JED. Fluorescent light. Shots with too much headroom. That's the next stage.

RICHARD. That's it?

ADAM. Go on, Jed . . .

JED. Well . . . I don't know, maybe the wings are in here somewhere, our shoes on the patients, but barely noticeable yet. And on the doctor I thought like softer shoes, comfortable walking versions, maybe . . .

RICHARD. Sure, why not?

ADAM. And the next stage?

JED. We see the same people, the patients, obviously, but the doctors too, and they . . . now they're jogging, playing football, squash, training. They're active. And, there's a slogan.

RICHARD. What slogan?

JED. 'Herpes Can Be Beaten.'

RICHARD. They're still wearing the shoes?

ADAM. Of course they're wearing the shoes.

JED. 'Can't Beat Mercury.'

RICHARD. I can't believe this is happening.

JED. And then the final stage. Whatever the disease, we always put out just the Mercury Wing, simple, and the tagline: 'Almost Anything Can Be Beaten' – i.e., not Mercury.

RICHARD. YOU THINK IT'S A GOOD IDEA TO ASSOCIATE OUR SHOES WITH VENEREAL DISEASE? What kind of goddamned philosophy is that?!

JED. The idea is that even when you hear about herpes, read about herpes, see herpes, contract herpes –

RICHARD (*overlapping on 'contract herpes'*). Jesus . . .

JED (*continuing*). – you think of our shoes.

ADAM (*overlapping*). Adversity advertising. It's triumph over adversity, isn't it, Jed?

RICHARD (*overlapping*). How could you do this to me? It's outrageous.

JED. It's supposed to be outrageous. I think it's a good idea. Sorry.

Pause.

I don't feel very well. I'm sorry.

Pause.

ADAM. It's okay. Good. Do you have anything more?

JED. No. That's it.

ADAM. Okay. Great. Thank you.

JED. That's all?

ADAM. Just for now, yeah. We'll talk tomorrow. Get some rest, Jed, you look like death.

JED. Yeah. Okay.

He exits. Silence.

ADAM. Well.

RICHARD. Adam . . .

ADAM. He's your boy.

RICHARD. He's unwell, Adam. I don't know what the fuck that was, but it's not advertising.

ADAM. You don't think that's the kind of thinking we need?

RICHARD. Adam, come on . . .

ADAM *gets up and dumps his files into a wastepaper basket. He keeps a large envelope.*

You can't really think . . . ? He's an amateur.

ADAM. Sit down, Richard.

He hands the envelope to RICHARD.

RICHARD. What's this?

ADAM. I'm leaving. I'm leaving Mercury.

RICHARD. Fuck you. You're upset.

ADAM. No.

RICHARD. You don't think –

ADAM. Richard, listen to me. You can have first shot at my shares. There's a promissory note in there for a cash or paper sale between us or –

RICHARD (*overlapping*). You can't . . . Oh fuck, Adam. Not your little artist girl?

ADAM. *Don't.*

RICHARD. You're going to chuck it all in because of some new girl?!

ADAM. Not *because* of her.

RICHARD. No? What then? Just a flash out of the blue? A sudden decision to fuck me up the ass and screw the fortunes of our life's work?

ADAM. I need a new challenge.

RICHARD. Oh, here we go –

ADAM. The collection –

RICHARD. Fuck off.

ADAM. I'm going to rearrange my portfolio to support the collection.

RICHARD. You can't. You have obligations, Adam.

ADAM. I've made my decision.

RICHARD. WHAT ABOUT ME?! Who the hell's gonna do your job?!

ADAM. There's always someone.

RICHARD. You think I don't get tired and afraid sometimes?! So you didn't come up with the greatest idea of all time this round, so fuckin' what! What are you gonna do? Join the seminary?

ADAM. I'm going to Colorado.

RICHARD. Jesus Christ Thoreau, to what? Plant fucking beans or something? I'm trying to help you! I've always had to help you because you don't know yourself. Can't you see that, Adam? You can't leave me, Adam.

ADAM *says nothing*.

I disown you, do you understand me? I disown you.

Silence.

Please . . .

ADAM. Too late.

He exits. RICHARD *alone in silence. After a moment, he goes to the wastepaper basket and retrieves the files. He opens the first and stares at it. Considers. He goes to the phone; considers . . . Finally he picks up the phone and punches a button.*

Scene Twenty

Late at night. ADAM *is lying on the floor of the Amedeo Gallery. His shoes sit beside him.* NADINE *enters. She watches him for some time.*

ADAM. How long have you been standing there?

NADINE. Not long.

ADAM. I did it. I left.

NADINE. Congratulations.

ADAM. I feel nauseous.

Little pause.

When we were kids, we played a lot of tennis. I won some tough matches, but I was inconsistent. Whereas Richard was perfectly consistent, he just never won. Put us together and we took every tournament going.

Little pause.

Let's fuck right here in the middle of the floor.

NADINE (*producing files*). Your brother gave me these.

ADAM. What?

NADINE. Your files. Your ad campaign ideas.

ADAM. Nadine . . .

NADINE. Or should I say my ideas?

ADAM. Remember Richard's very pissed off with me at the moment.

NADINE (*reading*). 'Mercury Shoes: We're in Your Video.'

ADAM. It's just a sketch.

NADINE. When were you going to tell me?

ADAM. I was never going to use it. It was inspiration. I threw it out.

NADINE. Is this what's going to happen to my work?

ADAM. Nadine. You're upset. I understand.

NADINE. When the show's finished. Is it going to Chicago?
Or New York? I hope it's New York.

ADAM. You're not ready for New York.

NADINE. Which leaves Chicago. Or maybe one of your
houses.

ADAM. It's going into storage.

NADINE (*beat, then*). That's what I guessed.

ADAM. You knew that.

NADINE. I thought you liked it.

ADAM. I do, I love it. I *bought* it. I don't want to break it up.

NADINE. It's not one piece, it's everything I've ever done.

ADAM. But I see it as –

NADINE. You're not the artist.

ADAM. What's important is what you do next, Nadine.

NADINE. I made a mistake, Adam. I'm sorry. I'd like to
arrange a *droit en suite*.

ADAM. I don't know what you mean, Nadine.

NADINE. Resale rights payments; you do. Or maybe Jennifer
can arrange to ship my work back to me.

ADAM. But I'm not selling.

NADINE. Please, Adam.

Pause.

ADAM. Don't blow this, Nadine.

They stare at one another.

I want you to be part of my life. I do. Don't pretend you
don't understand because it's difficult.

NADINE *exits.*

Scene Twenty-One

MARY *in the cupboard at Mercury Planet. She is dressed entirely in black and sits with a shoebox on her lap.* JED *enters still wearing his suit. He stares at her and the shoebox.*

MARY. Jed.

JED. I'm not here.

MARY. I didn't think you were coming.

JED. Is that . . . really . . . ?

MARY *nods.*

MARY. Where were you . . . ?

JED. I've been walking around . . . just . . . Thinking. Mary.

MARY. You've cut it a bit fine.

JED. I'm going to call the police. (*Beat.*) Now. (*Beat.*) I'll wait with you.

Pause.

MARY. You need to take this upstairs, Jed.

JED. Did you hear me?

MARY. We don't have very long.

JED. Mary.

MARY. You're so close, Jed. I can't get up there, but . . . All you have to do is take it upstairs to the office. Slide it under the desk . . . You can do it, Jed.

JED. I don't think you want this either. It doesn't mean we can't do other stuff.

MARY (*looking at watch*). I don't think the police could even get here.

JED. Mary . . .

MARY. Can you feel it, Jed? This is life without packaging.

Setting down the box.

JED. Wait. Don't.

MARY. You can't be in both worlds. We all want to believe it, but that's the lie. You have to choose.

JED. Don't, Mary. Please.

MARY. I'll wait for you in the park. (*Checking her watch.*) Good luck.

She exits. JED stands alone with the shoebox. He gingerly lifts the lid. It's full of wires, a timer and a single running shoe . . .

Oh fuck. No.

He begins to breathe heavily. He looks to the door, around the room, back to the box. Suddenly he lashes out, screams, throws his arms about in a kind of wild explosive fit.

Blackout. An intense explosion of sound or music, harsh and extreme, but not a literal explosion. In the darkness, the noise develops into the sounds of a hospital, which fade to introduce:

Scene Twenty-Two

A figure lying in a hospital bed, eyes closed. Eventually he wakes, and slowly looks about. It's JED. He buzzes for a nurse. Nothing. He looks about.

JED. Nurse?

He buzzes again. Nothing. Looks about.

Hello?

He buzzes once more. Nothing. He closes his eyes. Pause. MARY enters; she wears dark sunglasses and a headscarf, her hair a different colour: either a wig or a new cut. She stands a long time at the foot of the bed. Eventually JED opens his eyes. He stares at her. Long silence.

The angel of death.

Pause.

Nice look. Who you supposed to be? Miranda Richardson in *The Crying Game*?

No answer.

Where did you go?

No answer.

Was it a test?

MARY. You tell me.

JED. Fuck off. I just about blew myself up.

MARY. No you didn't.

JED. I could have.

MARY. Why are you still here?

JED. I WAS IN A COMA.

MARY. You passed out.

JED. I thought I was having a heart attack.

MARY. Panic, I heard. And asthma.

Pause.

What did you tell them?

JED. Who?

MARY. You know who.

JED. I don't know. I was pretty delirious. There've been a lot of questions.

MARY. What questions?

JED. Well . . . they want to know why I had a shoebox with only one right shoe, and why it had wires and fuses running through it like laces, all connected to an alarm clock and a whack of explosives –

MARY. They weren't connected.

JED. No, it turns out they weren't. The explosives weren't connected.

Pause.

I was a little surprised myself.

Still. The authorities remain a touch suspicious. Go figure.

MARY. What did you say?

No answer.

What did you – ?

JED. Fuck all. I told them fuck all. I said I was working late. I went in there to think.

MARY. They believed you?

JED. I don't know – shall I call them? They're the ones outside my door in the uniforms.

Little pause.

MARY. You already called them once, didn't you?

JED. Were the explosives ever connected?

MARY. Why didn't you go upstairs?

JED. They weren't, were they?

MARY. Why didn't you just take the box into the offices?

JED. Because it was completely fuckin' insane, what do you think?!

MARY. You were so close, Jed.

JED. I was trying to help you.

MARY. You have an answer for everything, don't you? An opinion. Just no conviction.

JED. *Would you like to hear my opinion about you?*

MARY. You have so many ideas, ideals even, but they're flapping around in the wind 'cause they're so close to the surface. (*Pointing to her head.*) Up here. (*Touches her heart.*) No ideas here.

JED. You need help.

MARY. Did your life flash before your eyes?

JED. No. What about you? When you were sitting in the park, did anything go through your head? Did you imagine me, or us, or were you just looking for smoke on the horizon?

MARY. I couldn't do it.

JED (*beat*). What? Blow me up?

MARY. I guess, yeah.

JED. Well. That's good.

MARY. Is it?

JED. Isn't it?

MARY. I don't know.

JED. You think you should have blown me up?

MARY. Maybe I should have stayed focused on the big things.

JED (*beat, then*). That is the most fucking egotistical thing I've ever heard.

MARY. Is it?

Pause.

Jed. I need to know if you're going to say anything.

No answer.

Jed –

JED. No. I'm not.

MARY. Okay. Me neither. I have to go.

JED. I did do it for you, you know. All of it. You can't deny that.

MARY. You didn't do anything.

As she exits, RICHARD *enters, dishevelled.*

RICHARD. Who's that?

JED. Oh no. This *is* hell.

RICHARD. Jed . . . ? It's me, Jed. Richard. Richard Amedeo.

JED. I'm not delirious. I know who you are.

RICHARD. You look like shit.

JED. I've had better nights.

RICHARD. Yeah, well, it must've beeen a full moon.

JED. You didn't need to come and see me, Mr Amedeo.

RICHARD. I did.

JED. It probably looks pretty bad.

RICHARD. I've already spoken to the detective.

JED. You have?

RICHARD. I told him you're a good guy. Great worker.

JED. Really?

RICHARD. They're very curious. He appreciated it.

JED. Thank you.

Little pause.

RICHARD. Caused quite a commotion, all this.

JED. Yeah, I guess.

RICHARD. I saw all the trucks from the window, heard the sirens.

JED. What?

RICHARD. I was upstairs. Had a sort of bad night.

JED. You were upstairs?

RICHARD. I thought of coming down, but then I thought, fuck it. *Fuck it*. Light my fire.

JED. Yeah . . .

RICHARD. This detective tells me they figure if you're not a terrorist you might be a hero.

JED. I'm neither, sir.

RICHARD. Got your call and found you using your body to shield the thing. Or passed out.

JED. My asthma.

RICHARD. They said panic –

JED. Well, I don't know . . .

RICHARD. The thing nobody understands is what the hell you were doing there, Jed. In the middle of the night.

JED (*beat, then*). Instinct.

RICHARD. You think?

JED. Or luck, maybe. Yeah. Working overtime.

RICHARD. Right.

Little pause.

JED. Was Adam still up there too?

RICHARD. Who the hell knows where Adam is, Jed.

JED. Sorry?

RICHARD. You can't trust anyone in this world. Not one goddamned person; it's every man for himself. Always has been, always will be.

Little pause.

Except for you.

JED. Oh. Well, like I said . . .

RICHARD. A real modern-day hero.

JED. Not really.

RICHARD. Yeah, really, Jed. A real hero.

JED. I don't think so.

RICHARD. There's a scrum of photographers out there desperate for your photo, did you know that? 'The Hero Released from Hospital.'

JED. Really?

RICHARD. But I got a better idea. Wanna hear it?

JED. Sure.

RICHARD. 'The President of Mercury Shakes Hands with Heroic Employee.'

He holds up a pair of shiny new Mercury running shoes.

I brought these.

JED. I don't think I can.

RICHARD. Sure you can.

JED. I don't feel up to it.

RICHARD. For me, you can, Jed. Put 'em on.

Pause.

JED. No. Sorry.

Pause.

RICHARD. Well. Fuck me.

JED. I'm sorry, Mr Amedeo.

RICHARD. There it is then, huh? Just like that. The last of the Mohicans.

He looks a moment at JED, *then sets the shoes on the bed.*

Your gold watch.

He straightens his tie, his hair, etc.

The whole world's gone crazy but it's gonna be hungover tomorrow. Not me. No regrets. I'm gonna go out there and tell them my man isn't fit to speak. He's traumatised, confused. He's weak. Then I'll take some questions about our new Mercury Planet and my vision for Mercury Shoes. You Can't Beat Mercury, huh, Jed?

Scene Twenty-Three

JED *and* NADINE *at home.* JED *sits on the bed in his pyjamas, the remnants of breakfast on the tray beside him. Flowers beside the bed.* NADINE *is getting ready to go out.*

JED. I like what you've done with the place.

NADINE *gives him a look.*

Well, you've moved things.

NADINE. You were gone for maybe thirty-six hours. Tops.

JED. In body.

NADINE. I moved stuff back, that's all.

JED. Thanks.

NADINE. Not for you. (*Changing her top.*) Turn.

JED. What?

NADINE. Turn.

JED. Oh, come on. Okay . . . (*He turns.*) You didn't have to take me back.

NADINE. It's your apartment too, that's all. I'm just trying to be . . . 'good', I guess. (*She has finished dressing.*) Okay.

JED. You know, after the explosion –

NADINE. There was no explosion.

JED. No, but metaphorically –

NADINE. Right . . .

JED. You feel like, *I* feel like I've woken up for the first time, you know, defied death or something. Sort of that morning feeling. Like maybe there's a reason.

NADINE. You didn't OD on placebos, did you?

JED. When I get better –

NADINE. The doctors say there's absolutely nothing wrong. You just panicked.

JED. It was a terrifying experience, you know.

NADINE. Yeah. I know.

JED. So, I mean when I fully recover, I'm going to do something.

NADINE (*putting on her coat*). I know.

JED. I am, seriously.

NADINE. I'm looking for a new studio, Jed. A cheap space I can live and work in. Somewhere I can concentrate again.

JED. You don't have to, you know.

NADINE *looks at him.*

No, I just mean. Because of me.

Little pause.

NADINE. I've got this idea for a new project. It's in a box, all these cards, file cards or whatever, and they can be taken out and hung all over a room, and on each of them is an idea for a piece of work, like: 'The artist will create a self-portrait through X-rays and other medical procedures' – and a price. And if you buy it, I'll make it for you. But not before. What do you think?

JED. Sounds good.

NADINE. It's just an idea.

JED. I'm sorry, Nadine.

Little pause.

NADINE. Yeah. I'm sorry too.

JED. I'll go.

NADINE. You don't have to.

JED. No, I will.

NADINE. It's okay, I need a studio.

JED. I will . . .

NADINE. Okay. Well, I've got lots of stuff to do today, so . . . I'm off.

JED. Nadine?

NADINE. What?

JED. Nothing. I want to make dinner tonight. That's all. Cook us dinner.

NADINE. Yeah?

JED. What do you feel like?

NADINE. I don't know, surprise me, whatever you want.

JED. It doesn't matter to me.

NADINE. I have to go. You choose.

She exits. JED is left alone. He leans over and smells the flowers beside the bed. Then he tilts his head back and drains the last drops of his coffee. He sits a few moments, deliberating. He lays back in bed, closes his eyes.

The End.

A Nick Hern Book

Someone Else's Shoes first published in Great Britain as a paperback original in 2007 by Nick Hern Books Limited, 14 Larden Road, London W3 7ST in association with English Touring Theatre

Cover image photographed by Manuel Harlan and designed by Jane Harper
Cover designed by Ned Hoste, 2H

Typeset by Country Setting, Kingsdown, Kent CT14 8ES
Printed in Great Britain by Bookmarque, Croydon, Surrey

A CIP catalogue record for this book is available from the British Library

ISBN 978 1 85459 980 3